JOURNEY TO ME
A Discovery of Self

Created by

Antoinette Pellegrini

Book 3: We Inspire Now Series

First published by We Inspire Now Books 2021

Copyright © 2021 Antoinette Pellegrini

ISBN
Print: 978-0-6487645-5-7
Ebook: 978-0-6487645-6-4

Antoinette Pellegrini has asserted her right under the Copyright, Designs and Patents Act 1988 to be identified as the author of this work.

The information in this book is based on each author's experiences and opinions. Each author retains copyright over their individual work.

Antoinette Pellegrini, as publisher through her business, *We Inspire Now Books*, specifically disclaims responsibility for any adverse consequences, which may result from the use of the information contained herein in the works by the other individual authors. Each individual author takes responsibility for their content and for any permissions to use information. Any breaches will be rectified in further editions of the book.

All rights reserved. No part of this publication may be reproduced, stored in or introduced into a retrieval system, or transmitted in any form, or by any means (electronic, mechanical, photocopying, recording or otherwise) without the prior written permission of the author. Any person who commits any unauthorised act in relation to this publication may be liable to criminal prosecution and civil claims for damages. Enquiries should be made through the publisher.

Cover image and design :   Antoinette Pellegrini

Layout and typesetting: Antoinette Pellegrini
                                We Inspire Now Books

We Inspire Now Books
PO BOX 133 Greensborough,
Victoria Australia 3088
www.weinspirenowbooks.com

Dedication

For anyone who has searched to find out who they truly are.

The answer is inside you.

The three books in the *We Inspire Now Anthology Series* were award winning finalists at the International Book Awards at the American Book Fests.

Book 1:   *Live Your Truth* (2019)

Book 2:   *A Message To Your Younger Self: What Would You Say?* (2021)

Book 3:   *Journey To Me* (2022)

Contents

Introduction: What Does It Mean To Be Me?	*Antoinette Pellegrini*	1
Finding My Fire	*Antoinette Pellegrini*	11
Chicken Coops and Collies	*Sothi de Boer*	25
Keep on Keeping On	*Johanna Elizabeth*	39
Control And The Year Of COVID-19	*Lesley Lennon*	55
The Traveller Life	*Sal Prothero*	69
I Don't Have Time For Cancer	*Lynne Owens*	79
Adventure After 50	*Heather Thorne*	99
Wings of Wonder; My Lessons of Journey	*Diane Psaila*	111
Weight Off My Shoulders	*Caterina Zanca*	135
Where To From Here	*Dawn Sulley*	149
I Have A Story To Tell	*Francis Borg*	167
My Money and Lipstick Story	*Suze Elford*	183
What We Discovered		205
Author Bios		223

Introduction

What Does It Mean To Be Me?

Antoinette Pellegrini

Who Am I?

This is perhaps the simplest question and, at the same time, the most complex and difficult to answer. What does it mean to say, 'I am being Me?' What does it mean to 'Journey to Me?'

These are questions that are explored by the co-authors in this book, and they all have a different interpretation. I believe being yourself is a process, a journey to become and be who you are.

Many of us have recently been exploring these questions. The COVID-19 pandemic which hit the world early in 2020 and which is still impacting us today in 2021, caused many to re-evaluate who and what was important to them.

In lockdown, many felt that the very things they took for granted, such as family, friends, and the freedom to do the things they love, were the very things that mattered the most. Many changed careers, moved away from cities and enjoyed the simpler, more creative pursuits in life. The questions: Who am I? What is important to me? What do I want from life?, were questions that many people around the world were asking.

So who are you?

In my first book, *Your Thoughts Matter: The Future You are Creating Starts Now*, I included a reflection entitled *Who I Am*. I wrote:

When asked who you are, do you state your name? That is often what is expected, but your name does not explain who you are. It is a title usually given to you by someone else. You can change your name, and many of us do, at various times of our lives. Your name is important, but it does not explain who you are.

You might say that you are someone's brother, sister, mother or father, wife or husband, but this explains a relationship – who you are in relation to someone else. It is part of who you are, but only a small part.

Introduction: What Does It Mean To Be Me?

You may define yourself by your occupation. You might say you are a student, a housewife, an office worker or doctor, but your occupation does not define who you are. It explains what you do at a particular point in time. Your occupation will change over time as you grow, develop, mature and retire.

Those who define themselves by their relationship with others or through their occupation often feel lost when the relationship or the occupation ends - like the mother who feels empty when her children grow up and leave home, or the person who always defined themselves through their job, retiring and feeling that they are now nobody.

None of these things explain who you are.

Are you your body? Your body changes every day, you age and your cells are constantly being replaced. You grow old, your appearance changes. Your physical body is a shell that contains you; it does not define you.

Are you your mind? You can change your mind and control your mind. You can decide what to think, do and act. You can decide how to react to the circumstances of your life. You are more than your mind, more than your intellect.

You are an emotional being with a myriad of different feelings and emotions passing through you every day, but even this is not all you are. You can control your emotions. You can decide to be angry or to calm down. You are more than your emotions.

You are a social, intellectual, emotional and physical human being, but this does not capture the essence of who you are. You are much more than this, something real, yet hard to define.

Who Are You? [1]

In *Your Thoughts Matter*, I concluded that at our core, we are all spirit, an eternal vibration of energy. My belief is that we are creative beings of energy, connected to, and part of, the universal energy that is everyone and everything. Yet, we rarely feel this, let alone experience ourselves like this.

The reality is that who we are is so often influenced by what others say, the expectations, beliefs and values of our parents and the beliefs we established for ourselves when we were young. Often these beliefs about ourselves are negative, limiting and often wrong. Yet, they often influence our decisions, choices in life and how we see ourselves, often for our entire lives.

Our beliefs about the world, including our personal limiting beliefs that don't serve us, are largely developed during childhood, before the age of seven.

Dr Bruce Lipton, American biologist and author of *The Biology of Belief,* [2] says that from birth to around age seven, you operate primarily in brain wavelengths that are very close to a hypnotic state.

This means that as children, we are literally sponges, soaking up everything around us, as we see it, without analysis or interpretation.

---

[1] Pellegrini, Antoinette *Your Thoughts Matter: The Future You Are Creating Starts Now*, Busybird Publishing, Melbourne 2017, pp 23-25.
[2] Lipton, Bruce *The Biology of Belief*, Mountain of Love/Elite Books, Santa Rosa CA, 2005

Some of these beliefs are supportive for us, but some very limiting, such as feelings that you are not worthy of love, are unwanted, or not good enough. These beliefs are formed as a result of the behaviours we see and by how we are treated by our parents, siblings, and other people we know.

These beliefs make up a lot of who we are and how we see the world, but they may not even be our beliefs. They may be beliefs imparted to us by others when we were young, beliefs that have gone straight into our subconscious, to be replayed again and again as habitual behaviours.

Sometimes, it may not have been the intention of the others to impact us negatively and impart such beliefs. A personal example is that for most of my life, I have felt that I wasn't good enough.

This limiting belief impacted almost every part of my life and my relationships. It was formed as a result of my father always exaggerating my achievements when he described them to others. It made me feel that no matter what I achieved, it wasn't good enough for my father. I don't believe he intentionally wanted me to feel this, but that is what happened, and it has taken me until 60 years of age to be free of that belief.

Perhaps the *Journey to Me* is not just about becoming who you are but unbecoming who you are not - only then do you discover, or more accurately, uncover who you are.

This concept was expressed by Paul Coelho in his famous quote:

> *Maybe the journey isn't so much about becoming anything.*
>
> *Maybe it's unbecoming everything that isn't you so you can be who you were meant to be in the first place.*

The process of unbecoming what you are not to become who you are, applied to this book itself.

Being part of my anthology series, *We Inspire Now,* wasn't the original intention for this book. It was meant to be an anthology for a Meetup group for women over 50, but that didn't eventuate, and this book happened instead.

I always find that books have a mind of their own, often starting out being one thing and becoming something else entirely – perhaps what they should always have been.

Unbecoming what I am not, has certainly been true for me.

How do I be ME if most of my life I have spent it being who I thought I should be, who my parents wanted me to be, who my partners wanted me to be, who I thought I should be for my children.

Retiring from my corporate job five years ago has allowed me the time to finally achieve some of the things I have always wanted to do – writing, publishing my books, running workshops and guiding others. It has been challenging and rewarding, and it is fulfilling my purpose, although in so many ways, I feel that at age 60, I have only just begun this journey.

But the question, Who Am I? remains.

What is the uniqueness that is ME? Are my beliefs and values mine, or were they given to me by my parents?

My spiritual beliefs are definitely mine. I rejected the religious beliefs I was brought up with. I didn't follow any set of established religious beliefs and developed my own version of spirituality – a mix of quantum physics and metaphysics, a combination of science and spirituality, that I use to make sense of the world. This is part of ME.

But to really become ME, I had to shed the limiting belief of not being good enough that I have held since I was young. It has taken me my whole life to achieve it, a journey that is taking me closer to ME than I have ever been before.

Part of this journey has been fulfilling my dream of being an author and helping others achieve their own purpose and find their voice. It is the reason I created this anthology series.

I believe that everyone's thoughts, feelings and experiences matter, and that the lives and challenges faced and overcome by ordinary people can and do inspire others.

We all have our own music inside us – something we love or yearn to do, our passion, our gift, our purpose. The music inside you is your gift to yourself but also to the world. Not pursuing the passion inside you also means not allowing the rest of us to experience your gift.

This is the third book in my *We Inspire Now* anthology series.

I was very honoured that both the first book in the series, *Live Your Truth*, and second book *A Message to Your Younger Self*, were award winning finalists in their category at the 2019 (Book 1) and 2021(Book 2) International Book Awards sponsored by the American Book Fest. It is validation that the stories of ordinary people from Melbourne could touch the hearts of people on the other side of the world.

All of the co-authors in this third book in the series, *Journey To Me*, share their personal stories, but in many ways, they are the universal story. You will see yourself reflected in at least some of the stories in this book. Some will resonate more with you than others, but it is my hope that they inspire you to take your own journey to be more fully who you are.

The 'Journey to Me' is a personal one and different for every person. We all live that journey in our own way. The challenges faced by the co-authors of this anthology are similar to those faced by many. Some of us, including myself, have experienced grief from the loss or separation from a partner and the subsequent challenges of raising children on our own. Some co-authors have experienced physical trauma, ill health, or mental trauma.

The authors share their stories about coping with the COVID-19 pandemic, finding themselves through their work, their family, following their passion, having the courage to move interstate, surviving cancer, losing weight or shedding limiting childhood beliefs. We have faced the challenges of feeling fear, insecurity, loneliness, not feeling good enough, yet these stories are ones of survival and achievement.

The biographies of all of the co-authors are at the back of the book. I encourage you to read about them and what they do.

The last chapter in the anthology called *What We Discovered*, provides a summary of the three key insights the co-authors discovered along their journey. This acts not only as a summary of what they have written about in their chapters, but as practical advice you can use to assist you in your own personal discovery and development journey.

I hope you enjoy this anthology and that it inspires you to take your own journey to unbecome what you are not, discover and be who you really are, whatever that means for you.

In so doing, you will inspire others to do the same.

Antoinette Pellegrini
2021

Finding My Fire

Antoinette Pellegrini

Uncover the real you and show the world your fire — who you really are.

Antoinette Pellegrini

I had lost my fire.

It happened gradually, and I hadn't even noticed – not until it was too late. My parents tried to take it away, and to some extent, they did. 'Do the right thing.' 'Think about what others will say.' 'Obey the rules.' These were constant reminders of the need to conform to what others wanted and expected. All of that was more important than being yourself, but it wasn't until the end of my first marriage that I realised my fire had gone.

After he walked out and left me devastated, I remember looking around the house and thinking that there was not a single thing in there that I chose, that I liked, or that represented me. Where had I gone?

I barely had the confidence to speak. It happened without my noticing – giving in to him, not saying how I felt, keeping the peace. Isn't that what I was supposed to do? But it had come at a high cost – a much higher price than I realised at the time, a price that I am only now starting to understand.

So, did I find myself back then? Of course not. How could I?

I was a sole parent with a three-month-old and a two-year-old to bring up. My needs didn't even bear a mention or a thought. It was about survival and doing the best I could for my boys. I was not a priority in my life.

Other relationships and even another marriage, came and went, and I wasn't truly myself in any of them. I loved the men I was with, but I entered the relationships quickly. The main criteria were that they wanted me and wanted to be in a relationship with me.

From a very young age, I felt that I wasn't good enough, but when these men wanted me, I found validation – I must be okay, I must be good enough. The fact that I didn't know them when I entered relationships didn't matter – I barely knew myself.

It wasn't their fault. My fire was buried deep and who they saw wasn't truly who I was. There were glimpses at times, happy moments, but it is not easy being happy when you are not being yourself or speaking up and saying how you feel about things.

I wasn't even conscious of how buried my spark was – even the work I was doing didn't satisfy me. I was earning a very good salary at a corporate job, but it was killing my soul.

What was I doing?

I felt that I didn't have a choice. I still had two boys to raise, private school fees and a mortgage that was increasing by the day to cover expenses that were beyond my means. I couldn't give up my job. I sometimes wonder if I made the right decision. The job cost me dearly, but it also cost my boys less time with me.

I thought at the time that the best thing I could do for them was to give them a good education, but I do wonder if they could have received that at a public school which perhaps would have given me the opportunity to do another job which would have enabled me to spend more time with them.

Instead, I was exhausted most of the time, working long hours at a stressful job. I felt I had to wait until I could officially retire. My boys are wonderful, intelligent and caring young men who I am very proud of, so perhaps I did okay by them.

I finally left the job in 2016. I still had a mortgage to pay, but my boys were adults and were working. It was finally my turn, and I decided to prioritise myself. I left to pursue my passion for writing and my drive to make a positive difference to the world – a grand inspiration that I had no idea how I would fulfil.

It was time to change, and that also meant leaving my 13-year relationship. There was not much left for either of us. I went to Europe with a good friend, and it was fantastic. I was free and doing what I had always wanted to do – travel, see new places, experience life.

When I came back, I met a man unlike anyone else I had met before. He was a dancer, attractive, flamboyant, charismatic and fascinating. He gave me his number and said he wanted to see me again. I dismissed it. We did see each other a few times at Meetup events. On New Year's Eve he tried to kiss me, but I stopped him. I was drawn to him, but I wasn't ready for him yet.

Instead, I reverted to old patterns. Four weeks later, I met a 'good Italian man'. He seemed steady, with a stable job, and he was very keen. He saw 'the nice girl', but he didn't see, and I didn't show him the fire inside me.

The relationship lasted almost three years. He wasn't the 'good man' I thought he was, and I wasn't the compliant woman he thought I was. I felt that I had to choose between him and my friends. He didn't like going out; he wanted to stay home, watch television, and look at Facebook. I was bored, itching to live, but I felt I was just existing. The relationship had to end, and it did, two days before the new year of 2020.

The COVID pandemic hit.

With it came isolation, and for me, a chance to re-evaluate what was important in my life. Who was I? What did I want in my life? I had already published three books and was on the path to finding myself, but it took a global pandemic for me, and perhaps many people, to take stock of the important things in life.

I grew, I changed, I embraced me. The fire was still there, waiting to emerge.

Perhaps it was no coincidence that in October that year, on a dating site, I came across the charismatic man I had met four years earlier. I thought, 'Should I send him a message? He probably won't even remember me.'

He did remember me, and we started what has been an emotional roller coaster ride.

It certainly hasn't been boring. I have found joy and fun. I am dancing again, something I hadn't done for many years, and we talk about everything and anything. We are similar in many ways, but it has also been challenging, difficult and emotional.

It was three and a half months into our new relationship, the middle of the night, and I was awake with tears in my eyes. The old triggers surfaced. He said he didn't want a relationship, yet it felt like we were in one. It didn't make sense. Was I not good enough for him? That feeling reared its ugly head again.

I had been working on clearing the feeling of not being good enough for over two years. I thought I was done with it, but no, I had felt it again numerous times over the first three months, that night it was there again.

The feeling that I wasn't good enough started when I was very young.

It was a belief I developed from my interactions with my father, yet he had never used those words. He had never said to me, 'You are not good enough', but his words and actions led me to believe that was the case.

I always felt that Dad expected me to achieve and do better than others, better than my sisters, better than my school friends. I tried my best to meet these expectations, but it wasn't who I was or what I wanted. I just wanted a big hug and to be told that I was loved and good enough just the way I was.

But no matter how hard I tried, it was never enough for my father. Whenever I achieved something significant, Dad would boast about it to others - family, friends and relatives - because for him, it was what others thought that really mattered.

The issue for me was that he didn't just boast about what I had achieved; he always exaggerated it - B became A, A became A+, best in class became best in the year level.

I remember a comment Dad made when one day when I was in my thirties. He had spent the whole day complaining I hadn't done things the right way. I was a sole parent at the time, and my boys were still very young. I was only doing my best, but that didn't seem to be good enough.

We were driving back from my father-in-law's funeral. My boys and parents were in the car when Dad made his latest complaint, 'Didn't you notice that the boys' pants have become unhemmed. They look scruffy.'

It was the final straw.

I snapped and started banging the steering wheel and screaming, 'Stop it! Why are you always criticising me? Why am I never good enough for you?' It was uncharacteristic of me, and he was taken aback. I still remember the surprised look on his face as he explained, 'It's just that I love you so much, and I want you to be perfect.'

I was deflated.

Obviously, I wasn't perfect in my Dad's eyes. It was confirmation that I wasn't good enough. I was never going to be good enough for him.

What I realise now is that Dad thought he was helping and encouraging me. He had no idea of the negative effect his words were having on me.

I remember as a fifteen-year-old, standing in front of a mirror, hating what I saw. I hated how I looked - I wasn't slim enough, I wasn't pretty enough, I wasn't cool enough or trendy enough – I just wasn't enough!

It was later in that year that I was to experience the first time a male showed interest in me. It set up a pattern that would last a very long time.

We met at a rehearsal for the school formal. The Catholic girls' school I attended was having a formal ball with the local Catholic boys' school. The boys visited for rehearsals, and we were all excited and a bit nervous. We were learning progressive dances, and it was fun. A few days later, one of my girlfriends came up to me to say that one of the boys liked me and wanted to meet me. I couldn't believe it. Me!

He liked me! Who was he? I had no idea.

I found out that he was the school prefect. He was popular, tall, good looking. I couldn't believe that he liked me, amongst all of the other girls. I agreed to meet him, and we went for a walk around the park. He asked me to be his partner at the school formal. We met up a few times after that, and it was all very innocent. We shared a kiss. It was my first kiss, and I will never forget it, but our relationship never went beyond this, mainly due to my feelings of insecurity and unworthiness.

What this encounter with a boy who liked me did was to start a pattern that was to continue for most of my life - a boy likes me, so I must be OK. I didn't feel good enough, but if a man wanted me, then I must be good enough in his eyes.

This became my criteria for entering relationships. If a man wanted to be in a relationship with me, then I agreed. I didn't wait to find out what type of man he was or whether we had compatible values. If he wanted me, that was enough.

In all of my long term relationships with men, commitment happened within one or two dates. Both of my husbands proposed to me within two months of our meeting, and in both cases, we were married within a year.

For both my marriages, it was only after we became engaged, the date set, and wedding invitations sent out that I started to find out who they were, and that our values and what we wanted from life weren't compatible. But it was too late then. I had committed, and I would try my best to make it work.

You would think I would have learnt from my first experience, but no, I didn't. I repeated the pattern – almost an exact copy.

In hindsight, that all sounds so foolish, but it didn't at the time. They wanted me, and that meant I was good enough for them. The pattern repeated with all of my relationships.

But now, I was with a man who said he didn't want a relationship with me, but he didn't want to leave it either. It didn't make sense. It triggered me, and although I had thought I had resolved those feelings of inadequacy, there they were again.

It was 3.00 in the morning, and I was awake with tears streaming down my face.

Then it happened - a switch was flicked, the light bulb turned on, a bolt came from the blue, it was the eureka moment – there are many clichés to describe it, but the feeling was real.

In an instant, something changed inside me. That 'not good enough' feeling was finally gone. I knew that I was good enough, and this is not dependent on anyone else or anything else. Being ME was all I needed to be, and that was more than enough.

I felt, I knew, that I was good enough, that I deserved more. I no longer needed to find my worth and validation through a man.

Finally, at age 60, the limiting belief that I wasn't good enough, that I had carried with me all of my life, was finally gone. Being ME was all I needed to be, and that was more than enough. That knowing remains today, despite the continued ups and downs in our relationship.

I felt euphoric. I knew who I was, and I knew my value. It didn't matter if he didn't see it, I saw it, and that was all that mattered.

I hadn't been ready to face all of this when I had met him over four years earlier, and neither was he. Covid and isolation had changed both of us, and we were both ready to transform and find ourselves. I realised that my boyfriend's actions and responses were also being triggered by his limiting beliefs and experiences from his childhood.

But the transformation hasn't been easy.

Over the past months, there were so many times I thought I should just leave, but I didn't; I couldn't. He said he didn't want a relationship, but he didn't leave either. He pushed me away several times, only to pull me back.

It is unlike any other relationship I have been in. I am not validated. He doesn't tell me I am attractive, but he often tells me how 'hot' his previous girlfriends had been. He doesn't tell me he loves me. He hasn't said he wants to be with me forever, like my other partners all did. He has said he would probably leave at some point.

Every other man had told me they loved me, found me attractive, sexy and beautiful. They wanted to be with me, make love to me, to be in a relationship with me, to marry me, to love me forever, and it was in those words that I had found my validation, my self-worth. Yet, the relationships didn't last forever.

Now I was with a man who said none of those things. He could so easily have devastated me; instead, the opposite was the case. Instead of sinking into an identity crisis, or feeling that I wasn't good enough, it has enabled me to see the truth, that the only place I will find self-worth is within myself – everything else is an illusion. I have now found my self-worth.

There was a reason we had met.

We had both been so hurt, and we carried the baggage with us, but we were also transforming and changing. About five months into the relationship, I realised that he was enabling me to go back to who I was before I was married – physically and emotionally, but without my limiting beliefs. I was starting to feel like I was 20 again.

My fire was returning.

I was finding myself – perhaps it takes the tumultuous, emotional rollercoaster to re-ignite the spark. It does make sense. You cannot change by repeating old patterns and doing what you have always done. Another man who validated me would not have forced me to fully face the reality of my patterns. He has taken me outside my comfort zone – a zone which, to be truthful, wasn't very comfortable.

I now no longer needed to find my self-worth through a man. I found more of me, I am unbecoming what I was not, and finally becoming who I am – it is liberating and empowering.

We have now been together for nine months, and we are both still changing and growing as people – becoming who we perhaps would always have been without our childhood limiting beliefs.

How long will our relationship last? I don't know, and I plan to take each moment and each day as it comes. Still, I will always be grateful to this amazing man and thankful for a relationship that has enabled me to grow, recognise and feel my self-worth, and finally become the real ME.

The spark is back, and the fire within me is burning.

I am excited to finally be ME, and that is definitely enough.

Chicken Coops And Collies

Sothi de Boer

Tell me and I forget.
Teach me and I remember.
Involve me and I learn.

Benjamin Franklin

Journey To Me

It is the mid-1960s. I live in government housing in my hometown of Kuantan in Malaysia. My father works for Telecoms. My mother is our educator.

The heat ripples float off the top of the hot bitumen as I jump off the school bus.

The federation green and yellow telephone booth tardis stands majestically at the intersection. The burning afternoon sun permeates up to my face as I eagerly charge home, school bag swinging freely on my shoulder while my imagination runs wild thinking of lunch.

'What is for lunch?!'

The wide steel gates conjure up the expectation of seeing a little boy swinging off them, to and fro. They lead straight into my home.

642 Jalan Temerloh Kuantan was one of a terraced row of eight houses, stuck to each other like biscotti, and these rows of houses were separated by a potholed, monsoon damaged bitumen road. Our eight double-backdoors exactly matched another set of eight double-backdoors across this road. The houses were cozily sandwiched together with thrown-cement brick

walls, and we were connected - kitchen to kitchen on one side and bathroom to bathroom on the other.

Our two-bedroom government-housing home was our sanctuary. Our neighbours were our village, and everyone looked after each other. This was where the seeds of multiculturism and racial tolerance were sown, and we grew up seeing no difference amongst ourselves.

We played cricket and football, backyard games with rattan and tennis balls and with sticks and stones. We collaborated on an annual sports day with distance running (around the eight houses, of course), relays, hurdles, high jump and long jump. We held football matches and badminton tournaments in which parents would referee or umpire.

My mother allowed us to have the family dining table and her best velvet tablecloth for the presentation ceremony. We collected the gold and silver paper inserts from cigarette boxes all year and shaped and moulded trophies for all the placings for each event. Guests were invited from adjacent streets, and they would arrive all dressed up in traditional clothes. We made flags, we had teams, we held a march, and we always had a VIP who would present the trophies. The fun we had growing up in such close quarters with so many people moulded us as citizens of the world.

Out the front of our row of houses was an expanse of land, and our eight front doors looked over to eight houses, all clinging together. On a piece of this land opposite our house, my father built a chicken coop.

One could not let the land go to waste. We had a flock of chickens and a couple of roosters, and plenty of chicken coop duties.

During this time, across the Indian Ocean, a teenage boy in another capital city of another continent is jam-packed into a Mini with a dog, a collie-kelpie cross, three brothers, Mum and Dad. So starts a two day trip from Canberra to Adelaide.

They used to live in New Zealand. Two of the boys were born in Winton, NZ. When Opa, Oma and the remaining five adult siblings of his mother's family wanted to migrate from the Netherlands, New Zealand refused them entry, but Australia accepted them as migrants. Consequently, his family left Invercargill in New Zealand and moved to Collie in Western Australia to begin a new life. Work was scarce. His father turned his hands to any job he could get. They opened a butcher's shop, had a milk run; he worked on the Wellington Dam and served in the Public Works.

The summer day in Elizabeth, Australia, was dry and brown as the car pulls in and brakes into the driveway. The collie dog is ready for a run. Another Air Force commissioned house for another three years. The house is like all the others - prescription defence housing that promises new adventures. Trixie curls into the normality of life as another day sets. There are expanses of scarce dusty bushland to explore on bicycles and rivers to jump into. Mum adjusts into another rhythm of Dad's work, our school, going for her driver's licence and entertaining them with sumptuous Dutch meals of aardappel, vlees and groeten (meat, potatoes and three veg), stamppot, hachee and brown bean soup.

'Feed the 'kollees(chickens),' booms my voice as I nervously realise that it is four o'clock and Papa will be home after work.

The Magnolia margarine tin is filled to the rim with vegetable cuttings and shavings, leftovers and the starchy strained water from today's rice pot, its jagged top hammered in to prevent cuts and hurts. I put the tin down and wrestle with the gentle, nostalgic garden gate held shut by a hooked wire. Straining to balance the spilling chook grits, I pour the swill into the ingenious zinc chicken feeders. The chickens scratch and peck their way through the sticky mess now speckled with sand from the floor of the chook pen.

'Shut that gate. Get those butts out of there'. My voice is authoritative and responsible.

I see the rounded cheeks of homemade pants sticking out of the ten by ten inch opening into the A-framed nesting henhouse. A shocked face swivels around, and a wide cheeky smile slowly spreads across the flushed, beautiful face. I extract him by the elastic of his pants, and squatting inside is another child.

The chickens sitting on the newspaper and hay watch unperturbed. Suddenly, 'paak, paak, pekaak' as one chicken lays her egg and flies to the exit. Chicken, feathers and child come flying out of the claustrophobic enclosure.

My school days began when I was seven. My father placed me across the front bar of a bicycle and pedalled off to a kindergarten that had opened temporarily in a house. Missionary schools prevailed in Malaysia during the 60s, and the Assunta Convent School was still being built.

I loved school, and I enjoyed learning. We all graduated to a Methodist Girls Secondary School where learning, leadership and responsibility were encouraged. I then had the opportunity to finish my HSC at Taylor's College. I applied to study in England, Australia and Canada and accepted an offer from LaTrobe University in Melbourne because Gough Whitlam promised me a tertiary education free of fees. For that privilege, I am forever indebted to Australia.

A child studying overseas is revered in my community and culture. I was a child who was given this opportunity.

I am a scholar. I am lucky. I am an investment. I was given a gift.

The financial burden on the family was immeasurable; my responsibility to successfully achieve my degree was enormous. Leaving home to attend University overseas was simply another passage in life. We were a middle-class family of seven steeped in community values and traditional conservative upbringing. There were no visible physical expression or demonstration of love or attachment in our family.

Now I am at the airport surrounded by family, extended family and trepidation, waiting to fly away. As I turned my back to wave them all goodbye, I saw my father tearing up. It caught me by surprise. He actually cared. I stopped, and I whispered to my Papa that I was going off to do something great.

The Malaysian Airlines aeroplane is dimpled with squarish lights, and the tarmac is busy with beeping and twinkling lights as ground handling staff load baggage and freight. I have never flown before. It is my inaugural flight.

What is this cardboard paper with my name, flight number and dots and dashes? What does it look like inside a Boeing 747B aeroplane?

Is that my seat number?

Do they show me to my seat?

Where did I last put my passport?!!! I never had one of those before, let alone ever needed one. It is a night flight, so it is quiet and sane. I watch the passenger next to me go through the rituals of overhead storage, fold-out table and blanket. I navigate my way through unknown territory while my companion looks like an expert.

The sunrise deflects off the cloudline, and the land below is brown and interspersed by meandering rivers, river terraces and valleys and flood plains. Lake Eyre lays dry and shimmering in the reflecting sun.

Melbourne reveals itself as we descend slowly into the sunburnt countryside so different to where I have come from. The dispersed housing leaves an indelible memory. All of my worldly possessions are in my one suitcase, as I begin my long-anticipated and elated liberation into university education, new friends and experiences.

The brand new 500CC Yamaha motorbike set against the eucalyptus landscaped farm on swampy river flats revs into action as the anticipated trip to the big smoke begins. He lives three hours away in the countryside of Gippsland. Life, with two gorgeous collies Rex and Scotty, has been totally focused on getting into tertiary education. These calm, perceptive companions have buffered and deflected disappointment, boredom and routine as they demand walks and attention.

Serena and I stand cowering into my winter coat as the wind swirls and hisses around us as we wait for the large theatre doors to open. Two tall, handsome men stand within sight. The doors open, and what seems like a thousand students swoop into the abyss of a hall. It takes a while for our eyes to adjust to the light, and we excitedly file up the stairs and settle into our seats.

They are going to sit next to us; those Thors are sitting next to us!

Unconsciously we strike up a conversation. They introduce themselves. One reads an airmail written in Dutch from his Swiss parents, and the other has Dutch parents.

Six months slip by, and I turn twenty-one. There is excitement and enthusiasm about organising a celebratory party, the first for our newly acquired friendship.

A hundred people turn up, and it is a wonderful night. I return to my residential room elated and buzzing. Browsing through my birthday card, I put a name to every one of the signatures except one. An elusive chicken scratch, that is what it looks like!

All of us get caught up in the rhythm of varsity. Life is mottled with lecture timetables, long, laborious laboratory sessions, tutorials and examinations. We pass some and fail others. We make friends and lose touch with some as we navigate the maelstrom of university life. We realise that some of our choices did not match our capabilities so we change professional paths and alter our destiny.

The first year at University drifts by with term Chemistry exams, an absent-minded professor for Botany who even succeeds in falling off the stage, a handsome lecturer for Zoology and prestigious computer languages like Cobol, Fortran and Basic in Mathematics.

As my first-year examinations finished, I realised that I could not afford to return home to Kuantan for the summer holidays. There were job listings posted on noticeboards around the campus, and overseas students stood around them as if our final exam results were published. Mine was at a motor mechanics within walking distance of my residential college, where I cleaned and dusted the workshop and the office and did their stocktake.

After two days, they shut for the end of the year. It was a meagre money earner, but it was my reliable assurance for public transport money to get to my other holiday jobs. A group of us stacked shelves in a supermarket, and we bravely walked to and fro through a cemetery, timidly supporting each other. I have packed biscuits, laughed along with butchers, served food, cleaned enormous houses and ironed rails and rails of shirts.

In the following years, the University began to hold conferences during the summer break, and we had to vacate our rooms with no place to go. After stashing boxes of books and clothing in the basement of the college, off I went with a fold-up bed under my arms and a backpack. I picked and bottled summer fruits and cleaned houses for rent-free occupation of their sunrooms. Early in the day, I worked in factories and supermarkets.

I guess I epitomised Friedich Nietzsche's quote, 'He who has a why to live for can endure any how.'

I chose Biochemistry and Microbiology for my second year and lost my two Thors to Botany, Zoology and Genetics. We did stay in contact because one of them had a car - a front bench seated green EH Holden station wagon with its trademark white tag. Bowling alleys, picnics in Mt.Macedon, bushwalks through forestry land, two-dollar pizzas and five-dollar roast chickens were all possible because we had a ride.

It was the fourth year of my university studies, and the young man of Dutch parents with a motorbike and a car began to make an impression. We chatted and shared similar interests and values. The Honours year was very challenging for Dolf, so I began to take an interest in his work, get absorbed in the science of his research, and assisted with laboratory investigations and results collation.

There was a flat-warming party in Barnes Way, La Trobe University, and as always, everyone was invited. Some hours into the party, the two Thors and a girl approached me and asked if I would share the flat with them. Really? Me?! I accepted the offer and loved my room. That Easter, Dolf's parents invited all of us to their farm for a traditional Dutch Easter celebration and holiday. This family and the young man left an indelible impression on me.

We had great camaraderie, and the four of us worked well together. I shared my whole life with them, including my cooking, my cleaning and my heart.

In 1977, while sharing the Barnes Way flat, Dolf's parents invited the four of us to their country home for Easter. This stay revealed steadfast family values and close sibling bonds, which I valued and that struck a chord with me. We both understood each other at a deeper level, and there was a shift in our friendship.

I graduated. Dolf also graduates.

I have to pack all my possessions. It does not all fit into one suitcase anymore and is a tedious, laborious chore. I come across my 21st birthday card. I sit myself down and nostalgically finger through all those signatures.

That unidentified chicken scratch signature belongs to DOLF!

I apply for more than three hundred jobs, and I get disillusioned by all the rejections. A vocation in my qualifications is rather elusive, and my opportunity to remain in Australia begins to start slipping through my fingers.

Now I cannot afford to live in Melbourne anymore. Dolf's parents kindly accommodate me in their country property while I have to present myself to the Immigration Department in Melbourne every fortnight to extend my temporary visa. I never lost hope that I will one day get my permanent residence.

Amazingly, I encounter strokes of luck in my pursuit of an Australian residency. Every fortnight I would catch the train from Sale to Melbourne and skip my way up the hill to the Immigration Department on Spring Street. There was always hope, and I never ran out of determination or tenacity. An astute, meticulous, compassionate and generous immigration officer was at the heart of my success and happiness. I had to secure a job with my qualifications, and boy, was that hard.

One day he says to me, 'Go get any full-time job.' I head downtown into a pub and secure a bartenders position, run back up that glorious hill and got that stamp that allowed me to remain in Australia. A full-time position in Coles HQ finally seals my permanency, and life begins to unfold into the dream I had hoped for.

As I continued to get to know Dolf even more I began to realise that he would understand, respect and meld into my family and culture really easily. His intelligence, music and sense of calm captured my attention, and I started to grow fond of his company and capabilities. The year we both finished our degrees was very challenging as both of us had great difficulty finding jobs.

Dolf left Victoria looking for work, while luck was on my side, and I found a full-time job. He returned to manage a nursery for two years. We decided to get married, and he moved into my rented flat in Armadale. He was now free to search and apply for jobs in his qualified profession.

Our relationship has soared despite separation by distance, meagre accommodation and finances, intermarriage prejudice and uncertainty, and race discrimination and bias. We have accomplished many firsts that many relationships will never ever encounter.

I married the boy who grew up with collie dogs and had a chicken scratch for a signature.

We now live in Nunawading, Victoria.

Dolf is an Agricultural Research Scientist, and I am a Medical Scientist. Our children, Sunita, Anucia and

Rohen, have taken us on journeys not published by travel journals, challenged us with making decisions tailored for us and us alone and supported us to enjoy life. They are our guiding lights to a life we live well. They have had their hands on the rudder directing us through all forms of tides and storms, enriching our lives and definitely loving us unconditionally.

No more chicken coops for me. All collie dogs, black and white and golden brown.

Keep on Keeping On

Johanna Elizabeth

 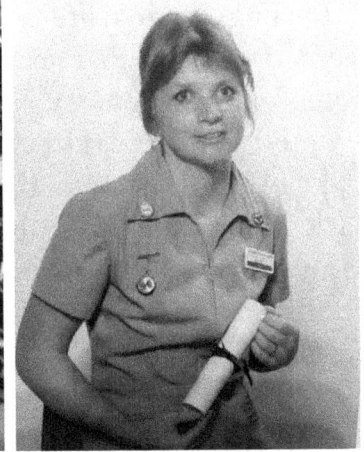

*Just put one foot in front of the other, and keep going.
You can do this.*

Johanna Elizabeth

'Mum, you've got balls,' my 14-year-old son said to me, as I attempted another renovation, or was it changing jobs? Or maybe it was when I was buying another investment property. I really don't remember exactly why he said those words. Funny how you can remember some of the things people say, but not necessarily why they said it.

Reflecting on my life at that time, I guess I always seemed to find that extra push in me to get things done. With that energy, although sometimes very tired, I would push on. How or why I could muster that extra effort was beyond me at the time, but looking back at it now, it probably was due to the power within me. I had grown resilient over the years and developed the determination not to surrender to my negative self-talk.

Born in the front room of a double story red brick house in Utrecht, Holland, now called the Netherlands, I was my parent's fifth child. Mum had a midwife deliver me; that's what they did back then. First child in hospital, if all went well, the others would be delivered at home by a midwife.

I was born 12lb, poor mum, on a sunny Wednesday afternoon at 5 pm. I was not planned, nor was my older brother born one year earlier. My father, born in 1911, my mother, 1913, married in their early twenties. Mum's family ran a delicatessen, and Dad's family a bakery or was it a pastry shop? They had three sons and two daughters.

In 1939 when World War 2 started, Holland surrendered within a few months. They were a very small country and were in the crossfire from Germany to England. After the surrender, the Germans would search the Dutch homes for the men to work in their factories during the war.

Mum told me the German soldiers were generally okay, it was mostly just a job to them, but it was the Gestapo soldiers who were cruel and ruthless. My father would hide in an upstairs cupboard that was hidden behind a bed. He eventually got caught and was taken to work in a German factory.

Now, mum was on her own with three children.

While I was growing up, my mother would frequently tell me stories about the war and how she watched the Germans hunt down the Jews, put them on trains, like cattle and taken away to be gassed to death. I hated her telling me these stories, she was always so graphic, and it scared me. I still get that horrible feeling when it gets talked about.

But as the war continued, food became very scarce. Mum would have to walk miles and miles to get food for the kids. There were food vouchers, but it was not enough. This was when she started selling her expensive paintings she inherited from her family. They would rent a room out to a boarder for more income. Yet still, there was not enough food. My eldest brother had on occasions taken the food meant for the rabbit; he was so hungry.

One day my brother heard that there was food nearby. He and my sister went up the road, near the Germans, there was a scuffle, and gunshots were fired. He ran home without my sister who was only six years old. Soon after that, a woman knocked on the front door, carrying my sister in her arms. Initially, mum thought she had wet her pants, but on closer inspection, it was clearly blood. They took her to the hospital. The bullet went straight through, very close to her ovary. Thankfully later in life, she still produced three children.

After the war, mum became unexpectedly pregnant with my brother, who was born quite sickly. One year later, I came along. My mother was 40 years old by then. My sister was more like a mother to me when I was little, and my eldest brother, like a father. Dad was a bit of a party boy and womaniser and was hardly ever home. I later married a man just like him.

Mum and Dad decided to start a new life for the family in sunny Australia. There was a lot of promotion at the time to lure migrants, offering very cheap fares to migrate to the land of opportunity.

Mum and Dad packed some furniture and possessions for the six-week journey on the ship 'Johan Van Oldenbarnevelt'. Dad loved the cruise across the world, really enjoying his time. Poor mum was very seasick and stayed in her room most of the time. I was frequently put in a creche and remember the little cubby in the corner where I would hide. I was scared and missed my family.

We first landed in Fremantle on the 12th February 1956, on Mum and Dad's wedding anniversary. We finally landed in Melbourne, where we were transported to Bonegilla, where we only stayed for a couple of weeks.

Our final destination was Broadmeadows army barracks on Camp Road, where we were given a Nissan hut made of corrugated iron. It was in the shape of a tin can, split down the middle. Three rooms for seven of us, and it was like an oven on a hot day. There was a large cafeteria where all the migrants went for meals and a communal bathroom for all to use. I remember having a potty under my bed; I was only four.

My mother was very sad and homesick; she missed her family and friends. While my dad, older brothers and sister went looking for work, I was put into a creche, and my brother put on a bus to go to school.

I remember crying and being scared, behind a fence, strange country, strange language, strange food, and people I did not know; I felt abandoned and lonely. I realise now how depressed my mother was. I cannot remember what Holland was like. Maybe a vague memory of snow and a sled my oldest brother had. The creche and the migrant camp were my first vivid memory of the start of my childhood.

Seven months later, we moved to a rental house in Glenroy. Dad found work as a painter decorator, my eldest brother in cabinet making, my middle brother got a job at Berger Paints, and my sister became a live-in babysitter. Life was looking up.

Dad got his licence, bought a car, and we were more mobile. We were a typical Dutch family in the 1950s. Dad was dominant, mum subservient, and the boys in the family were allowed much more freedom than the girls.

I still remember mum would say, 'The girls aren't allowed to eat meat; it is for the men. They are the breadwinners'. So I rarely ate meat while I was growing.

I started school at Westbreen state school, in the 'babies' grade, as they called it back then. I was bullied because I could not speak English, wore different clothes and ate different food.

I remember standing against the wall while the kids laughed at me. I ended up catching hepatitis A, probably because back then, all the toilets were 'dunny cans'. We had an outback toilet in our backyard, and I distinctly remember we could not use the toilet at 830am Thursday mornings. That's when the dunny can man came to replace the full one with an empty one. He carried it on his shoulder.

Eventually, Dad saved enough money to buy a block of land on Pascoe Vale Road, Glenroy. It had a small bungalow on it. When we moved there, we only had a tap out the front. My weekly bath would be in a tub. My mum would boil some water, wash my brother first, then it was my turn. After that, she would do the washing in the same water.

We were poor, I wore hand me downs, had long hair always in a ponytail, and I was very much a tomboy.

I started making friends with some children near where we lived. My brother and I were always out and about till dark. Mum was still sad most of the time, and her asthma was becoming more of a problem. I remember she was hospitalised, and that was one of the few times I actually remember my dad doing housework and helping us kids.

Mum and dad were not around all the time, my other two brothers and sister were working, so it was difficult growing up in this household. I was frequently left on my own or with my brother, who had become a bully towards me.

My childhood taught me a lot of survival and coping skills. I learnt when I was on my own to dream, plan and distract myself from what was going on around me. I developed a strong will and a determination to keep on keeping on. My tomboy style also gave me the confidence to explore. It made me more resilient than the girly girls at school.

School was easy for me. I was bright enough to sail through most of the subjects. My desire was to become a teacher. But this was cut short when we moved from our house in Glenroy to a house in Westmeadows when I was in the fifth form (leaving certificate).

The new house was a bus, train ride and a long walk to school. I did start my matriculation year, but the travel and my disruptive household caused me to leave at Easter time and start a job as a laboratory assistant for the Australian Wool Board in North Melbourne.

That was short-lived, and after several other jobs, I worked in an office on a billing machine. One of the first programmed machines. By now, I was seventeen and had a boyfriend who had a car. Although I had more freedom, I still had to be home by 10:30 pm during the week and midnight on Friday and Saturday nights.

Mum and Dad wanted me to get married as soon as possible and were not happy when I broke up with him. But he really was just a friend, and I was incredibly green and naive where boys were concerned.

Eventually, my brother set up a blind date for me, and that's where I met my husband. A bit of a lad with a hot car. A bad boy with a charming personality. He had been around, and I was a very green 19-year-old.

I learnt a lot about boys then, and within eight months, we were married. We were 20 years old. Back in those days, you would never live with someone before marriage.

Sadly I learnt a lot of painful lessons during our marriage. He was not faithful, nor was he very honest, and initially, I was so gullible I would believe anything he told me. He was always out while I was at home waiting. We were married in July 1972, and in October 1972, he confessed he had been having an affair. I wish he had never told me.

I remember him saying, 'Why don't you get bigger boobs so you'll be more sexy.' Luckily I went to a surgeon who asked me why I wanted bigger breasts. When I said, 'It is for my husband', he responded, 'Come back after you have children and see how you feel then.' With all the put-downs, I blamed myself. My self-esteem was so low.

To get through those years, I would write in my journal, which would also be a cross-check for some of the events that went on.

As the years rolled on, more truths came out about what he had been doing with his time. Eventually, I could not believe anything he told me anymore. He would always say after our arguments, 'I will change.' 'I won't do it again.' And then there would be chocolates and flowers the next day.

We had two boys together at this stage. He was rarely home, so I started to study and completed my H.S.C. (matriculation) – four subjects over three years.

My husband resented the time I was spending on my studies when he was home, so to reduce intimate times with him, I always tried to go to bed early and pretend I was asleep. After ten years of disruption, pain, and many arguments, we finally separated.

The initial time of separation was difficult. The boys were only two and four. It took a while to sell our home and for me to buy my own small place in Sunbury.

Having had so much time on my own, I had developed a lot of hands-on skills, like painting, building and decorating. We did not have a lot of money, so I was becoming more resourceful and independent. Having had a dad and brothers who were all handymen, I learnt a lot growing up.

I started dating again, and after several brief relationships, I met a lovely man. He was seven years younger than me. He was an up and coming solicitor who treated me like a princess, and he was so kind to the boys. He gave me back my confidence and self-esteem.

I was such a mess in my head after my marriage, with trust issues and self-doubt. He was just what I needed to get myself into the right frame of mind. He encouraged me to enter tertiary studies, as I had become a state enrolled nurse during my marriage, although broken up into halves, with six months after the birth of my first son and six months after my second son. There is more to this story, but that will be for another day.

I always wanted to become a registered nurse. I needed something to challenge me, as I was no good at mundane tasks. My life had been such a roller coaster that I was hooked on the adrenaline that came with stress. I knew I never wanted to be like my mum; I wanted to be an employed, independent parent for my boys to look up to. I wanted to give them a good education and the opportunity to become what they wanted.

I commenced my three-year Diploma of Health – Nursing course at Phillip Institute of Technology. It was not easy. I had to find suitable babysitters for the boys, who by this time were becoming lovable rascals but little live wires. We went through a few babysitters before I found Marilyn. The boys did not really like her, but she was reliable and had children with times that suited her to pick the boys up from school.

I was accepted to do my graduate year at the Heidelberg Repatriation Hospital, which had its challenges. From there, I went on to do my Rehabilitation Course at Royal Talbot in Kew and Fairfield Infectious hospital.

Prior to this, I had been on my own again. I broke up with the young solicitor due to all my insecurities. I met a man who lived around the corner with his parents. He had been married twice before, been through bankruptcy, so had no money, had estranged children, and a storeman's job. So certainly not someone I wanted to get serious with. But he was fun and good with the boys, and before I knew it, we were in a relationship, and later, he moved in, paying me a board of a lousy fifty dollars a week.

We moved to Mill Park into a new house that I bought by extending my loan. This move was necessary as the travel from Sunbury every day was too tiring. Once there, my boys went to the local Catholic school, a close walk for them.

Whilst during my 12-month Rehabilitation Course, I accidentally fell pregnant. It was the last thing I expected. Such a tiny percentage chance, but it still happened. I felt as if this is what God wanted for me for whatever reason, so there was no going back. Being a Catholic and with strong pro-life beliefs, I continued my course until I was seven months pregnant. I had my daughter and returned to work when she was only two weeks old, which was extremely difficult to do.

The clinical teacher just added time to the end of my course. I needed to do this as her father could not afford to pay to maintain our household. I started to resent him, as he was more of a child than a supportive partner.

Our daughter was four years old, and I asked him to leave. It was never supposed to be forever, but due to our beautiful girl, I hung on for as long as I could. The separation was ugly. Even though he was only a defacto, he took me to court in an attempt to get as much out of the relationship as possible.

During this challenging time, my father became ill with lung cancer and later died. Not that long after, my 20-year-old nephew, who lived in Queensland, drowned tragically. Around the same time, my sister was diagnosed with brain cancer as well. My mother was also deteriorating and died five months before my sister passed away. My sister tried so hard to stay; she was only in her fifties.

After these four deaths in my family, within a few years, my life was the worst it could be: three children, so much grief and stress. I started to get depressed and needed counselling. This went on for quite a while.

I still had to work, as I had the mortgage and the children's school fees. I started my job with the Royal District Nursing Service just after my father had passed, where I stayed for fifteen years. I even continued my studies - the RDNS Community Health Certificate, and with my experience with death and dying, I also completed a short course in Palliative Care at Peter McCallum Hospital. Later I completed a 12-month course in Stomal Therapy at Mayfield, and a Continence Certificate with RDNS.

I became hooked on study to get me through the stress that I was under. It sounds a bit crazy, but it was what I needed at the time. I would be so tired at night; I would set my alarm clock at 3 am to complete my assignments. My kids had to put up with me hiding in my room sometimes just to get my studies done.

All this extra study while working with three children gave me the distraction I needed. It kept me on the path of keep on keeping on attitude. As my son would say, 'Mum, you've got balls.' I was getting stronger. I even bought investment properties. But it was when I started my Masters in Gerontology, that the cost and time it required was just too much.

I grew very tired. The light, my inner strength or power inside of me, was diminishing.

After fifteen years at RDNS, in many roles, including working for the homeless for a year, I moved on to a palliative care unit in a hospital. Working part-time now was all I could manage. After about eight years, I finally burnt out.

I wasn't sleeping well with the shift work; my blood pressure was getting higher as well as I was just damn tired. I had run my race. Everything was such an effort. I needed to leave before I made a mistake. There were bullying issues at work as well, and I knew some just did not like me. I had to learn to accept that and move on. Nurses are great with patients but not so good with their colleagues - not always the case, but generally true.

On looking back over my childhood, marriage, study, relationships and work, I realised I had been pushing myself and spreading myself too thin. Still, my survival instincts always kept me going. I remember a friend telling me, 'Why do you make things hard for yourself?' I believe it was because I liked a challenge, and keeping busy helped me get through tough times.

During my years as a palliative care nurse, I found that the one thing that kept people hanging on was a strong will or strong survival instincts, compared to others that gave up too easily.

So if you have a strong disposition that keeps pushing you to achieve, you no doubt will hang on when the going gets tough. It is a quality to be admired. Even when tired, just put one foot in front of the other and keep going. Do not listen to that negative self-talk that can haunt you when trying new experiences. Push it aside and motivate yourself with the mantra, 'I can do this. Everything will be alright.' It is what I did.

I had also developed the art of surviving by short-circuiting a lot of false, needy and toxic people. The Dutch have the reputation of being outspoken and a bit abrupt. These mannerisms I also had developed in my role as a nurse. It helped to get to the important facts and problem solve quickly.

I had become very good at time management. Nurses are always so busy and pushed for time. My home life felt the same, with the children's sport, school activities, social commitments and domestic duties; it was the most hectic time of my life.

I learnt to value my free time, going for a walk in nature, breathing fresh air and walking on green grass in bare feet. I rewarded myself by going on holidays when the kids were with their dad. I also learnt that it was okay if someone did not like me, as long as I liked myself. I believe it may be spiritual guidance or an inner power that kept pushing me, but it was there, and it gave me strength and helped me be true to myself.

Now my children, who are all doing well, are adults, with lives and children of their own. They ask me, 'How did you do it, Mum?' I usually say something like, 'It was keeping so busy that helped me cope, as well as the distractions and sometimes the help of a supportive person, whether a friend or counsellor'.

I believe that my inner power and the desire to improve myself pushed me to keep going, as did my positive self-talk, 'I can do this', and 'Everything will be alright'.

Control And The Year Of COVID-19

Lesley Lennon

Life is not meant to be easy, but we can choose how we view challenging situations.
Lesley Lennon

As I start to write today, I look out the study window at my garden with a sense of anticipation. The sun is out, the sky is blue, and the leaves are beginning to come back on the big old oak tree. The seasons are changing around me as they are changing in my life. My eldest daughter has just gone into labour with her first baby, my first grandchild. I think, 'How weird is this, my baby having a baby?'

It seems like yesterday, but it is over thirty years since her birth. Even now, I can recall the emotions I experienced on that day. It was a mixture of excitement, joy, and fear. I remember feeling anxious about the uncertainty of what the future could bring. I thought, 'Will I be a good parent? Will I know how to look after my baby?' I wanted to have control and certainty over every aspect of my life. I still do. The events of 2020 have made this even clearer.

My 2020 year started well. For my husband Steve and I, this was reflected in the stock market. It was booming, and I felt a sense of comfort and stability. Each day Steve would pull out his Smartphone and say, 'Look at this flow chart Les. Look at the upward curve!' Despite not understanding the stock market, I knew enough to know this was a good thing.

Steve continued to say, 'We're going to be in a good place financially, Les.' I believed what he was saying, but I kept thinking, 'Is everything going to stay the same until we reach the age of retirement?' This was a big ask. Nonetheless, I nodded my head and smiled, hoping our future would be safe and nothing would prevent us from fulfilling our dreams.

We both had worked hard to raise our three children, who were now independent adults. I thought, 'It's now time for us to have some fun.' For me, fun meant freedom to catch up on all the things we had missed out on in our youth.

Steve and I started dating in year 12 when we were both eighteen and nineteen years old. 'Life is not meant to be easy,' I can recall Malcolm Fraser, our Prime Minister in 1971, say. For us in 1984, this was definitely true. There was no Gap year or time to have fun. We both finished High School, found full-time jobs straight away and then married and bought our first home two years later.

That is when Steve started his corporate life, and I thought, 'Great. Stability and a regular income.' Little did I realise the impact corporate life would have on him and our relationship. Often over the years, I would say, 'Steve, you're like a robot. You feel no emotion.' And he would say to me, 'Les, you're too emotional and get upset too easily.' The circumstances of 2020 only served to highlight our differences.

By 2017 after 32 years of working in the corporate world, Steve found it difficult to continue. Although the work had been financially beneficial, it had left him feeling physically exhausted and mentally drained. So, when he was offered a redundancy package, I said, 'Grab it!' He had mixed emotions. On the one hand, he was excited at the prospect of freedom, and on the other, he was afraid of the uncertainty not having a job might bring. 'Everything will be okay.' I said, 'It is what we have been dreaming of.' I, too, was quietly sceptical and thought, 'Is this too good to be true? Are we really going to have the freedom we have been wanting and waiting for?'

My intuition must have been telling me something. By February of 2020, the media started reporting about a highly contagious virus Scientists named Covid19. The reports told us the virus was sweeping through China at a rapid rate, and thousands of people were becoming very unwell. 'Gees,' I said to Steve, 'This is unbelievable.'

But like most Australians at the time, we both continued with our daily routines without giving the reports too much thought. That was until one day, while I was doing my grocery shopping, I noticed some strange behaviour. I saw people frantically filling their trolleys with all sorts of tinned foods, rice, and flour.

One woman had nothing but packets of toilet paper in her trolley. 'What's going on?' I asked a worker who was busy restocking empty shelves. 'Is there something I need to know about? He said, 'No. There's nothing wrong with our supplies. I'm not sure why people are acting so crazy.' I shook my head, thinking, 'Something's going on.'

A few weeks later, I understood what was happening. It was a Sunday night, and I sat down with a coffee to watch the *60 Minutes* program. The entire program was on the Covid19 virus in China. I sat with my mouth agape as I watched. I could not believe the graphic images I was seeing. I felt sick. I saw people being barricaded in their apartment buildings against their will. I was mortified.

The reporter was saying, 'People with Covid19 are not allowed to leave their homes.' The vision showed overcrowded and chaotic hospitals. The reporter continued to say, 'Hospitals are unable to keep up with the influx of sick people, and thousands of people are dying.' As he left the hospital, he and the camera turned a corner to show hundreds and hundreds of body bags.

I could not believe what I was seeing. All the while, I'm thinking, 'This is happening far away. It could not happen here.' But I was sure now that this was why people had been crazily stockpiling supplies. They thought it would happen here just as it had in China.

I tried to convince myself the virus would go away, but the virus did nothing of the sort. Shortly after watching the *60 Minutes* program, my son Facetimed me from his home in the USA. He said, 'Hi Mum. I am okay, but the Covid19 virus is getting bad here. We had a thousand positive cases today.' 'No!' I screamed in my head. I was afraid for his wellbeing.

It was then I realised the virus could potentially affect my family and those I loved. I could not control the situation, and I felt panicked.

My first thoughts were, 'How can I protect him and keep him safe? What can I tell him to do?' The truth was I didn't know how to keep him safe. The visions from the *60 Minutes* program were on replay in my mind. All I could do was pray, 'Please Lord keep him safe.' Even then, I did not believe we would be affected in Australia.

That was where I was incredibly wrong. The virus began to rapidly spread throughout the world, and before long, we had our first few cases here. Australia's response was far different to the USA and other countries. Although they went into lockdown, it was only for a short period of time. It seemed to me they viewed the economic cost as being too great and far more important than the health of their people.

Within a short space of time, our Covid19 case numbers reached fifty, and our Victorian Premier, Daniel Andrews, called for an immediate lockdown. At the time, I was grateful and glad our Government appeared to care about our health despite the economic repercussions. I thought, 'It won't be for long. We will be able to control this thing.'

Initially, I did not understand what lockdown meant. But it soon became clear it meant every business, shop, café, and restaurant had to close its doors. No one could go to work unless they were an essential service worker. Everyone had to stay home. I kept telling myself, 'It's okay, it won't be for long.'

Again, I was wrong. The lockdown in total went for over seven months. It felt like what I imagined wartime to be like. There was no room for choice. We had to listen to the medical experts and politicians, and we had to wait for them to sort out our future. More and more restrictions were put in place. I had no control over the situation, and I felt powerless. 'What if they get it wrong? What if the virus is never controlled or eliminated?' The what-ifs were growing and playing on my mind.

The timing of the lockdown, in some ways, was fortunate for Steve and me. A few months before lockdown, we decided to renovate and move into a small one-bedroom apartment. At the completion of the renovation, the apartment, although small, was beautiful. It had a gorgeous garden, and I felt sure we would be fine there, given we had a busy lifestyle and were not home all that often. I thought, 'Life's rather good.'

But lockdown changed all of this. Steve and I were forced to stay in our apartment together for twenty-two hours a day. We were unable to see anyone, and eventually, the old issue of us not being emotionally connected returned. I kept thinking, 'I want my old life back.' The thought of this time being 'our time' was a distant one, and our future seemed uncertain.

As the lockdown continued, I learned more about the virus, and as I did, my levels of concern increased. It soon became evident that the elderly and the ill were the main victims of the virus. This instantly made me think of my elderly mother, who was living in a nursing home. I had not been able to visit her for months because of the strict Covid19 lockdown laws, and knew because of her Alzheimer's, she would not understand what was going on. I feared she would pass away during the lockdown, and I would not be able to see her again. 'Please angels, keep her safe,' I begged.

I was becoming mentally fatigued from the powerlessness I felt. I could not do any of the things I once could, and I felt frustrated and overwhelmed.

Another blow was soon dealt when my son and his girlfriend had to cancel their planned visit to Australia from the USA. Our Covid19 numbers were continuing to rise, and one way our Prime Minister, Scott Morrison, thought we could control the spread of the virus was to close all our borders to international visitors. Australian citizens could return but would need to go into mandatory hotel isolation for 14 days. I was now thinking, 'When will we see them again?' The uncertainty was unbearable.

Every day was now becoming a struggle. Even though scientists worldwide were trying to produce a vaccine, I knew it would be a long time before it could be implemented. I kept thinking, 'Please let there be a miracle breakthrough that will get us back to normal.'

The daily news reports were depressing, and I had to push myself to get out of bed. I felt that apart from my grandbaby's upcoming birth, there was not a lot to look forward to. I needed to talk to myself constantly and say, 'Come on, you have to keep going. Stop letting this thing get you down.'

Politically in Australia, a lot was going on. Initially, the State and Federal Governments seemed to be working well together. However, as time passed, the divide between the two became more apparent. Eventually, the Prime Minister started to take a back seat, and each State Premier began to independently deal with their own Covid19 situation.

It was not long before each State had their own set of regulations. For us in Melbourne, our restrictions intensified. We watched as other States began to reduce their case numbers and with them their restrictions. A sense of renewed freedom emerged in those states, and living in Victoria became almost intolerable.

I would ring my sister in Sydney, and she would say, 'I'm catching up with girlfriends at a café today,' and my auntie in Adelaide would text me saying, 'I'm off to the Barossa Valley for a few days, Les.' Knowing other States were living with more freedom was difficult. 'Why us?' I thought. 'Why can't we be free too?' I began to feel isolated and lonely.

As our case numbers in Victoria continued to rise, I began to worry even more about my mum. A lot of the cases were now occurring in Aged Care Facilities. Mum's home had not been infected, and I prayed every day, 'Please let her be safe and well.' Being unable to visit mum, the aged care home offered Zoom sessions which I was grateful for; however, it was clear she did not understand what was going on. I just kept hoping the case numbers would decline enough so that restrictions would be lifted, and I could go in to visit her. I longed for the day I could say, 'I love you, Mum,' and see her face light up in response.

As it turned out, my prayers were answered, and the restrictions were briefly lifted. I was ecstatic and could not wait to visit her. I had so much to share with her, and just seeing her in person allowed me to gauge how she was. The visit was brief and very controlled. Mum and I had to sit 1.5 meters away from each other, and we could not hug. As soon as I saw her, I smiled and said, 'Oh Mum, it's so good to see you.'

Remembering back to that day, I can still see myself incessantly talking. I chattered about the impending birth of my first grandchild and old times. 'Mum, do you remember when you used to make the beautiful fruit cake with the pink icing?' I asked, and she smiled and nodded her head. I came away from the visit believing she looked healthy, happy, and comfortable. 'Thank you, God, she's okay,' I said to myself as I left.

I did not know that this would be the last time I would see Mum alive. The following week she died suddenly and what was to follow was an unusual and difficult time of grieving for us all. Though there were few interstate flights due to the restrictions, my sister and her husband were able to fly down to Melbourne from Sydney. Both were masked and gloved, and I could barely recognise them when I picked them up at the airport. 'Is that you, Sheryl?' I asked, half-jokingly. We were lucky with the timing, as a few weeks later, flights were stopped altogether.

The funeral was far different from what I had always planned in my mind for Mum. It was small due to the restrictions with less than 15 people. 'I'm sorry, Mum,' I thought to myself. 'This is the best I can do for you.' Many of Mum's friends and relatives were unable to attend, so we live-streamed the service.

For my husband and me, my mum's passing was another of many stressful situations we had to face in 2020. I was joint executor with my sister, who was based in Sydney, and for practical reasons, the responsibility for looking after Mum's estate and financial affairs were left to me. I was deeply saddened and often thought, 'Why me? It is not fair.' My sister was unable to help empty Mum's room in the Aged Care Home, take her clothes to the Salvation Army, prepare her townhouse for sale, or organise the entombment of both Mum and Dad's ashes. I felt overwhelmed and burdened.

These and many other tasks relating to Mum's affairs weighed heavily on my shoulders. I looked to Steve for support and strength. Steve, however, was already suffering from the loss of a close friend who had passed away suddenly less than four days prior to Mum's death. I could see Steve was struggling to deal with everything we were experiencing. The old pattern of emotionally disconnecting continued, and we both became distant from one another.

Every day there seemed to be some event that added to our stress. After many months of lockdown, the Victorian economy, like the rest of the world, was in disarray. Most people had no control over their lives or financial affairs. We were no different. Our once seemingly prosperous superannuation portfolio did not quite look the same. The once upward curves of the stock market were now downward, and a great deal of our net worth had been lost. The sense of comfort and stability I once felt no longer existed.

Our future was no longer bright, and our feeling of having control over our future was disappearing. Our financial belt was severely tightened. Like most people, we were forced to apply for Government assistance. I kept thinking, 'What next? What else is going to be thrown our way?'

The answer to my question came in August 2020. The stress caused by the seven months of lockdown, coupled with the grief associated with the death of both my mother and our close friend, caused Steve and me to decide to separate. We both recognised the need to take some time apart from each other to focus on our individual healing. We both were sad, but we knew it was for the best.

Alone in my apartment, I tried to come to terms with the changes that had occurred in my life throughout 2020. I could never have foreseen what had occurred. 'I just can't believe what has happened,' I said to myself.

The time alone allowed me to see I needed to feel as though I had some control over my life. I then acknowledged I could either sit in my apartment and do nothing, or I could be proactive and seek change. Being in lockdown, the only way I could think to do that was to use the internet to find new friends and explore new interests. I told myself, 'I need to reset and find out what I want from my life going forward.'

While searching the internet, I found a site dedicated to linking people and their particular interests together. I was drawn to Meetup groups that focused on spirituality, personal development, Reiki, writing and friendships. I joined many groups and attended many online meetings. At the same time, I found Instagram groups that focused on similar areas of interest. Each source led me to books and websites, and soon my journey of healing and self-awareness began.

After a few months, I started to feel good about myself, and both my mindset and physical health improved.

Now, after many months of lockdown and as I finish writing, I look out my window once more and see the brilliant sun against the blue sky. The wind is blowing, and the branches on the big oak tree are swaying. It reminds me we have almost weathered the storm. My grandbaby has been born, and my life has evolved and changed. At this point, the case numbers in Victoria are now below ten, and we are working towards a plan to reopen our economy.

The events of 2020 have given me a new perspective on life. I am now more grateful for the things I once took for granted. Things like travelling, eating out and visiting family and friends, I will treasure with more intensity. I no longer take for granted the ability to have a choice, and material possessions hold even less importance to me than they did before. It is the people in my life I value most, and the time I can spend with them is precious.

Covid19 has made me realise that circumstances cannot always be controlled, but our perception of them can. I am grateful for the opportunity Covid19 has given me to learn more about myself, grow and challenge the way I viewed and lived my life. I am thankful for the opportunity Steve and I have given each other to heal.

I believe Steve and I will always be together; however, our life going forward may be lived differently than initially planned. We may decide to continue to live apart, or we may choose to live together. There is no rush to decide.

Covid19 has taught me to go with the flow of life rather than try to control the outcome. Valuing the time and precious life we have is what is most important.

The Traveller Life

Sal Prothero

Your struggles develop your strengths.

Arnold Schwarzenegger

Journey To Me

I love a good story. I'm not particularly good at telling a story but am enthralled at listening to a good one. Ireland is the land of storytellers, so maybe it's in my blood.

I spent my childhood in Ireland with my single mother, childminders, aunt and two cousins who were of similar age to me. Regrettably, my mum was always working to pay the bills and put food on the table. As an only child, I craved company, and my high school years were spent at boarding school, where my school friends were my second family.

I was a rebellious teenager and felt like the black sheep of the family. Feelings were 'pushed under the carpet' – we were seen, not heard. Trapped in the confines of backwards Ireland as it was then, I felt that no one listened to me. I longed to live in a free country where you could be the person you wanted to be, and no one stared at you if you looked different. My 6 ft height was a reason for people to stare, and my unique fashion sense was out of place in a conventional country.

In the 1980s, a racing driver or fighter jet pilot were not on the careers list. Why did I want a career that wasn't achievable? Leaving school with no idea about my future, my mum strongly encouraged me to do a year's secretarial course. I thought to myself, 'There's no way I will ever work in an office!' I did complete it as I felt it to be my duty; after all, I knew my mum secretly wanted me to do a degree.

Adventure beckoned. I left Ireland behind en route to Paris with a friend I had met at secretarial college. We were going to live and work there. I loved the French language and thought I could speak it reasonably well. The reality was quite different. We struggled to find a job, and my French was not as good as I thought!

We said to each other, 'Where will we go now?' My grandmother lived in London, so this looked like a logical destination with somewhere to stay for a few weeks. London was the place to be. Creative, cultural, buzzing, and you could be and look how you wanted (nobody stared). I loved it and took full advantage of it. I felt free living in London, after the restrictions in Ireland.

The secretarial course that I originally didn't want to do enabled me to leave the hospitality industry behind and work in the corporate world. After all, the hours and salary were better. I loved the marketing environment that I worked in, but the deadlines were stressful, and I couldn't handle the stress very well. I was able to keep going by drinking too much coffee, alcohol, refined carbohydrates, sugar and having a busy social life.

Along the way, I met my future husband in a nightclub. Dancing was one of my passions. Our friendship grew, and seven years later, we married. My biological clock was ticking, but London was not the best place to bring up a family.

My mum was living in Scotland at the time. On one of our visits, she said, 'Why don't you live here?' We said, 'No way, it's too cold!' Before we realised what was happening, my husband found a job in Stirling in Scotland. I had never heard of Stirling, but it didn't matter. We found ourselves living in a remote farmhouse with no neighbours nearby and no friends. My husband was a city boy. He struggled with the remoteness, but I loved it. I grew up outside a village by the sea so was used to country living.

It was a lonely time at first, like it is when you move to a new country where you don't know anyone. My husband had a career, but I was feeling lost. There was no corporate world there and no guaranteed job, so I applied to become a tour guide for a tourist bus company. Even though I wasn't a Scot and knew nothing about the history of Scotland, they offered me the job. I couldn't believe it!

Soon after, I found out I was pregnant. I couldn't work on a moving bus while heavily pregnant, could I? What if I fell down the stairs? My cautious doctor had told me to take it easy and not be 'Too active'. Being my first pregnancy, I took him at his word and my life as a tour guide was doomed before it even started. At least, I still rode my motorbike, but finally, common sense took over, and I stopped riding six months later.

We moved to a rural town to be nearer civilisation, and I worked part-time at the local real estate agency. I knew I couldn't work in real estate for the rest of my life and wondered what I could do that I would still enjoy in 10 years' time. Horticulture and interior design came to mind, but after discovering how diet and nutrition had helped with my various health issues, including anxiety and depression, this was my calling.

Living in a rural town meant there weren't any opportunities to attend a university or college. Distance learning was the only option. Heavily pregnant with our second child, I signed up for the Nutritional Medicine degree. I needed to do something for myself. How hard can it be? I would study while my baby slept during the day and after both kids have gone to bed. How naïve was I? I can remember getting my assignments in on time in an exhausted haze.

I loved the Scottish landscape and the people, but the weather really got me down. We didn't have much of a summer, and before we knew it, it was autumn until a harsh, cold winter hit again. The weather, along with my husband working away on many occasions, led us to make the tough decision to leave after eight years of living there. When my husband and I were thinking of which country to move to, Canada and Australia were the only English speaking countries we could think of at the time. Canada lost out due to its cold weather.

Sydney was always going to be the place I wanted to live in. In my 20s, I fell in love with it when I was there on a working holiday. When we finally received the approval to emigrate, actually doing so was heartbreaking as our kids were born there, and my mum, whom I'm close to, lived there. But the thought of living in another country beckoned. We thought we'd give it a year and move back if it didn't work out.

The prospect of moving to the other side of the world, leaving family and friends behind, was daunting, to say the least. Before we knew it, we were packed up and flying to Sydney, leaving the Scottish summer behind. Sydney's winter was like Scotland's summer! My kids were swimming in the sea, which drew attention from the locals. 'They must be mad; it's freezing!' were the usual comments.

Hubby was working and meeting new work colleagues, but I was alone, navigating my way around a new city, my daughter's new school and my son's day-care. I felt like a fish out of water. We lived near the sea, and the weather was fantastic. Warm weather was very welcome after the Irish and Scottish grey skies and damp bleakness, but I wasn't used to extreme heat and humidity.

However, ten months later, we were on the move again when hubby was transferred to Melbourne with his company. I was devastated. I still couldn't believe our luck at the opportunity to live in Sydney. After all, this was the place I wanted to live. Or was it? Sydney is an amazing city, but I was starting to wonder if it had any more to offer other than sun, sea and sand.

We arrived in Melbourne in the winter of 2009. Again, hubby's life hadn't changed dramatically as he still had work and a social life. My life involved looking after the kids and trying to make new friends. I desperately wanted to finish my degree and help other people who had been through a similar health journey. The drive to follow my passion and do something for myself was still there.

One day, when I was wandering around the CBD, a sign saying *Endeavour College of Natural Health* caught my attention. I thought, 'This is it,' this is a sign telling me to finish my degree!

Before I knew what I was doing, I signed up for the BHSc in Nutritional Medicine. As the degree was so different from the British one, it meant starting all over again. A mature student in my early 40s! I was old enough to be some of the students' grandmother! Being a student, wife, and mother was the toughest thing I've ever done. Being a new, temporary resident, we had little support in the way of friends, child support and no family to fall back on.

In 2015, I finally graduated. It took me ten years to finish my degree – from when I was pregnant in Scotland to finishing it in Melbourne. If I had known it would take that long, I would not have started. I'm not that crazy! However, it was my first degree, so I was very proud that I actually finished it. I couldn't believe that I was finally on the road to starting my own business and helping other people.

After 12 years of living in the same suburb of Melbourne, my kids were now teenagers, and my life had moved on from school pick-ups and school mum socialising. My new life revolved around attending small business network meetings. There, I met some of the most wonderful women, and some of them are now my good friends. We had a bond in that we all ran our own business and knew how tough it could be.

My business was operating on and off since the start of 2016. Who knew how hard it would be running a business doing the finance, invoicing, accounts, admin, social media, building relationships, being heard amongst all the other health and wellness noise. This didn't stop me, as I had worked hard to get where I was, and I wasn't going to give it all up.

During this time, my daughter became crippled with anxiety and depression later. It was a difficult time. Our lives consisted of psychologists and doctors' appointments, attempts at changing her diet, taking supplements, and dealing with the everyday traumas that anxiety brings.

As a mother, all I wanted was for my child to be happy. I became too involved in trying to 'fix' her that it took its toll, and chronic stress, burnout and depression reared their ugly heads. I experienced firsthand how inadequate the mental health system is and how lonely it can be if your child doesn't fit into the psychologist/medication piece of the puzzle. I also learned about the staggering number of kids who suffered from anxiety and depression and were unable to attend school. I discovered the statistics that aren't mentioned much in the media.

Did you know that depression is the number one cause of non-fatal disability in Australia? Did you know that the World Health Organisation estimates that depression will be the number one health concern in both the developed and developing nations by 2030? Kids as young as 11 are on anti-depressants, and Covid-19 has changed the world forever.

I found my calling. I had to specialise in mental health.

2020 saw a renewed focus. I offered an online program, one to one consultations and education about diet, nutrition, lifestyle, gut and mental health. The consultations give a more personal approach, and we can delve deeper, for example, functional medicine testing, food intolerances and supplements.

Of course, there are so many other factors involved in depression, anxiety, and mental health issues, such as environment, lifestyle, mindset, past and present stressors, biological processes but diet and nutrition still play a big part. My philosophy is to start with the diet and lifestyle – small changes make a big difference.

I worked on my diet and nutrition but didn't work on my mindset - who I am, what I'm capable of and what I want in life. I wanted to live the best life I could live. This involved daily gratitudes, affirmations and recognising my Human Design with a coach.

I had found me.

It is now almost a year since I first wrote my story. While reading it over, after the world changed from the Covid-19 pandemic, I wondered whether I should withdraw from this book. I felt that my message was unclear and questioned myself.

At a recent visit to my Kinesiologist, she asked me what happened when I was 42, as she felt it had been a significant time in my life. Upon delving further, I discovered it was the year I moved to Australia. It was such a difficult, challenging time, but I got through to the other side and don't regret it at all. I was meant to write this chapter.

We grow stronger from new and challenging experiences. I hope you have found some inspiration.

I Don't Have Time for Cancer

Lynne Owens

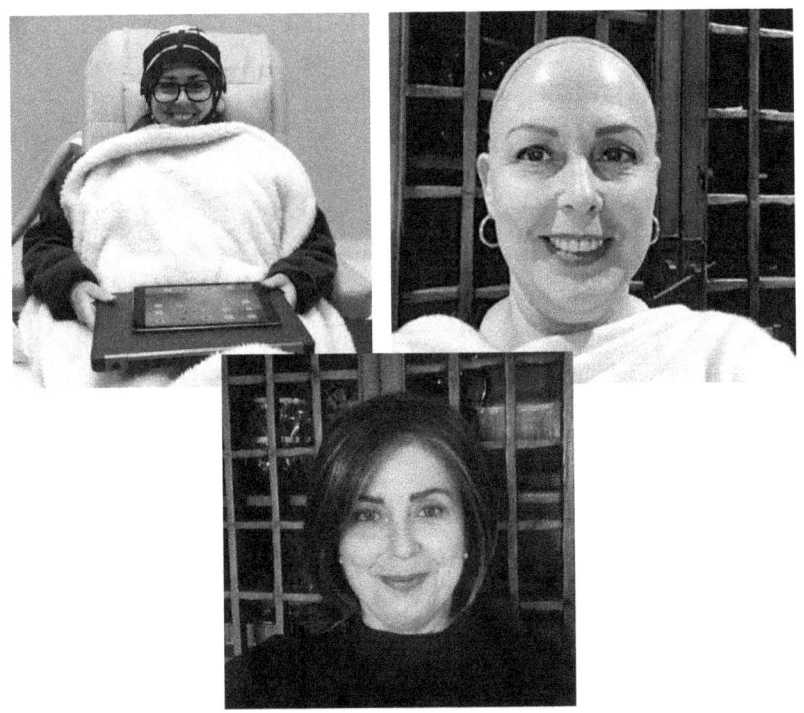

Never underestimate the power of the mind through illness.

Lynne Owens

Journey To Me

It was mid-October 2016. Life was good. Great friends, a job I loved, home renovation plans underway, and I was looking forward to a six-week Central American holiday at the end of the year.

I had recently celebrated my 52nd birthday and freshly returned from visiting friends in Hong Kong and shopping up a storm on our yearly junket across the border to Shenzhen, China. I had no idea my life was about to be turned upside down.

Here's a little snapshot about me. I am an incredibly private person who doesn't like to disclose information about myself. I am a self-sufficient, independent individual who doesn't like to ask for help. I am single and socially active, and an avid traveller. I am a full-time employee who commutes interstate most weeks for my job. I have mortgages to pay, I help care for my elderly parents (one with Alzheimer's), and I am a Reflexologist in my spare time. My life is pretty full.

Lying in bed, I was experiencing a dreaded hot flush, the kind that wakes you up in the middle of the night. My body was covered in perspiration, and I was in a frenzy to strip off all my clothing. When wiping away the perspiration on my body, my fingers brushed across my left breast and abruptly stopped, something didn't feel right, and on palpation, I felt a lump. Bizarrely, I wasn't alarmed and kept running my fingers over the lump again and again, trying to make sense of it. It felt big, not like a little bump under the skin; it was more like a large mass. Oddly enough, there was no tenderness. I was thinking to myself, 'How can something this big suddenly appear overnight? How could l not know this was growing inside me? How could I have not noticed this before?' Post hot flush and all cooled down, I eventually fell asleep.

On waking the next morning, the memory of the previous night's discovery popped into my head, and for a split second, I thought I might have just dreamed about it. I cautiously ran my fingers across the area, and sure enough, it was still there. I knew the right thing to do was to book an appointment to see the doctor. Yeah, right, it's a busy week; I will do that when I have time!

It was at least a week before I casually mentioned my newfound lump to girlfriends, and each time it was the exact same response, 'I'm sure there is no need to panic.'

'It's probably just a cyst; they are very common. I've had them.'

I wasn't convinced and knew I needed to make time and book that appointment.

I eventually saw the GP, and again, I was given the same response my girlfriends had given me, along with a referral to have a scan. As I was lying naked from the waist up on the table (a position I was going to get very used to over the coming years), the technician asked if the lump was painful to touch. I recalled the GP had also asked that very same question. My response to both was, 'NO.' I started to think it might be better if it was.

In my follow up appointment with the GP, we did the obligatory exchange of greetings before she read out the results to me, 'BARID 5 mass 4cm x 2cm, suspicious for neoplasia'. At that moment, I didn't register if this was good or bad news. In her next breath, she told me I needed to secure an emergency appointment with a surgeon as soon as possible. OK, I am now getting the picture.

She handed me a list of surgeons and suggested, 'Start calling first thing tomorrow morning until you get an appointment,' and that's exactly what I did. Finally, after endless attempts, I got through – hallelujah!

The secretary informed me in her matter of fact tone that I would have to wait at least three weeks. Not the response I expected to hear. I thought it was ludicrous and decided to take matters into my own hands. With scans securely lodged under my arm, I swiftly grabbed my handbag and car keys and rushed out of the house.

I arrived at the surgeon's room in record time, marched in and introduced myself to the secretary I had spoken with earlier and handed over all the information. Within minutes I was back on the road en route to the office. Before I had reached my destination, my mobile rang. It was the secretary I'd just met minutes before, requesting I come back in the morning to meet with the surgeon. Mission accomplished.

The surgeon was eccentric, professional and direct, 'Let's not jump to conclusions, but I hope you don't have any plans for the rest of the day; you're booked in for a biopsy.' I quickly rang the office to cancel my day and headed downstairs for the biopsy. The doctor and nurses were friendly and chatty, and I wasn't fazed by the procedure. They wished me good luck as they left me in the room to get dressed. I did ask myself why they were so nice to me. Is this how they treat everyone, or do they know it's something more sinister? I am now thinking, 'This is definitely no cyst.'

I met with my surgeon the following week. I sat anxiously in the waiting room for my turn. Finally, my name is called. Results were delivered, and it was now official - I had cancer.

Intuitively I already knew my outcome, but it still felt incredibly surreal to hear the words spoken - a little bit like having an out of body experience and watching some other poor soul getting the dreaded news that would change her life.

There were no tears, no meltdown or feeling sorry for myself; it was more like a multitude of questions swirling around in my head. Will I become sick? Will I look like someone who has cancer? Will I be able to function? Will I lose weight? Will I be able to work? And the worst thought of all, will I lose my hair?

The surgeon continued the discussion in a no-nonsense manner and talked about the type of cancer I had – who knew there were so many different types of breast cancer. Mine was a protein-based cancer known as HER2+, Grade 3, which means it was high grade and fast-growing. The good news was that I would not need a mastectomy. Instead, I would have restorative treatment, i.e. shrink the tumour with only a small amount of chemotherapy, followed by surgery to remove what was left of the tumour and surrounding tissue. Lastly, I would need to have a targeted therapy called Herceptin to destroy cells and reduce their ability to divide and grow. She saved the best news for last – I won't lose my hair!

This was music to my ears, and I felt tremendously relieved. This whole cancer business wasn't too bad after all, I thought. In fact, I left the appointment feeling quite confident it would pretty much be business as usual with no real impact on my life. The worst news was that I would need to cancel my upcoming holiday to Central America – I was shattered I couldn't go on this trip.

The next appointment was to meet with my oncologist, located in the same building as my surgeon – they often work together. He was a professor, slightly arrogant, very well-known and respected in his field. I was feeling quite positive about our first meeting, given the feedback from my surgeon. Alas, I didn't feel that way when I left.

The first thing he asked me was if I had a support person with me. 'No,' I said, 'It's just me.' Nobody had mentioned I needed a support person; I've never brought anyone along to a medical appointment with me before. Anyway, who was I going to bring with me? I was heading to the airport after my appointment.

He then got up from his chair and came around from behind the desk, walked to my side and sat down beside me, right up close and personal. I felt incredibly uneasy. He casually outlined his treatment plan for me – in a nutshell, it was going to be six months/16 sessions of unpleasant toxic chemotherapy with a list of hideous side effect to go with them, then surgery, six weeks of radiation, followed by another year of targeted therapy with Herceptin. Given I would need 40+ treatments, I would also need to have a port inserted into my chest, a Central Venous Internal Line, where the chemo had direct access to my veins.

I was trying to process what just happened. Why is he saying this to me? This is not what my surgeon had said. Surely, this cannot be right. The goalposts had been moved, and I was wondering how the hell I was going to fit this into my life. In my discombobulated state, I challenged him and his treatment plan, which didn't go down so well. He reminded me of his area of expertise and that I was welcome to get a second opinion. I was liking him less at this stage.

He then delivered the most devasting news of all, 'You will lose your hair; in fact, you will lose it after the first round of chemo.' Could my day get any worse – just stab me now. I didn't like him at all now!

This may not seem like a big deal for everyone, but for someone who has always liked her hair and was known for her long thick black hair, this was a big one for me. I could deal with the fact I was going to be a cancer patient, but I had no desire to look like one.

It was obvious that I was anxious about the hair situation, and he raised the option of using a treatment known as 'Scalp Cooling'. The machine allows cooling of the scalp with a continuous flow of coolant through a ridiculously tight-fitting cap. Basically, it freezes your head to save the hair follicles which are attacked by the chemo. No guarantee, but there is a 70% chance I may not lose my hair, and it may help promote future hair regrowth. No thinking music required, sign me up; I will try anything to keep my hair.

It wasn't all about the vanity; it was more about losing my identity and losing control of how I wanted to present myself to the world. I didn't want to be identified as a cancer patient. I wanted to get on with being me, the same person I was before my diagnosis, except I now need to find time to schedule in two years of treatment.

He suggested I take at least six months off work as it will take a toll on my body. I suggested that we wait and see how my body reacted and asked if I could still fly to work. He thought I had lost my mind!

I discussed this new development with my boss. He was compassionate and understanding, 'Take all the time you need,' he said. I didn't want time off; I wanted to work. I also asked him to keep my diagnosis a secret. The last thing I wanted was for staff to know my personal business and gossip behind my back. I was also concerned they may deem it too risky for me to commute and insist I take time off. As a single girl, I needed to work; nobody was offering to pay my bills.

I wanted to have a choice. I could allow this illness to be a battle, to be a victim, stay home curled up on the couch watching TV and feeling sorry for myself, or I could choose to surrender to the process and get on with the crazy ride. I opted for the latter. I became fiercely focussed and pragmatic in my approach of navigating the endless information, the countless appointments and tests and getting my head around what I was up against. There was never any doubt in my mind that I wasn't going to win this race; to me, it was just a hiccup, a bump in the road, and I was ready to drive straight over it to get to the finish line.

Over the next few days, I made a list of friends I wanted to share my news with. There was an assortment of responses from shock and disbelief, tears and encouragement.

I requested no posting on social media – I did not want people feeling sorry for me and sending me get well wishes for the world to see. I also conveyed my plan to step away from my social life for at least a year; I needed to focus on being able to work, and getting through the endless months of treatment that I was repeatedly advised would take a toll on my body. Most people (and doctors) assumed I would be taking time off and counselled me about what I should do. Let's face it; nobody likes to be told what they should do.

In the lead up to day one of treatment, I had two surgeries – the first was for the removal of my sentinel lymph node; fortunately, it had not spread. The second was to insert the port-a-cath into my chest. Thankfully mine was inserted deep into my chest and wasn't visible under clothing. It remained in my body for a little over two years. A good excuse to shop for new high neck clothing to hide my secret.

Two gorgeous girlfriends offered to drive me to the hospital. I was not allowed to drive through the first six months of treatment and happily accepted. There were no nerves, no tears, just a tenacious determination to get this done – the quicker I started, the quicker it would be all over.

The nurse who took care of me on the first day of treatment was the lovely Anna, who had conducted my introduction session; it was comforting to see a friendly, familiar face. At our introduction session, Anna told me the chemo would make me put on weight. Cancer was turning out to be the gift that just keeps on giving. Now I am going to be fat and bald!

Anna prepared me for the Cold Cap. She gently wet my hair and applied the conditioner, put on a tight skull cap, followed by a ridiculous looking helmet that buckled under my chin to hold it on tightly. The helmet was connected to the dreaded 'cold' machine.

In order for the Scalp Cooling treatment to work, you have it on your head an hour before chemo and an hour and after chemo – my head was literally frozen for six to seven hours a session. When they flick on the switch, a surge of cold hits your head, with the first 20 minutes being excruciating, like having a long, intense brain freeze. I gladly accepted the calming medication on offer. Not only was my head frozen, but my body temperature also dropped. I dressed like I was heading to the ski slopes. I was quite a sight. I can understand why some patients give up after the first session; it's not fun. As soon as the equipment was fitted to my head, I was desperate to get it off, but I persevered as I was even more desperate to keep my hair.

The process of administering chemo required more cross-checks than a flight attendant before take-off. I guess they need to ensure they were giving the right cocktail to the right patient. There were so many of us positioned around the perimeter of the room, a cross-section of ages, sizes and nationalities; cancer didn't discriminate. We sat around in our oversized chemo chairs, waiting for our turn, with absolutely no privacy. I hated that I was on show and always requested for the curtains to be drawn. I treated my small curtained off space as my office, with a laptop, phone and files around me.

The nurse used a numbing cream over the port-a-cath, then methodically cleaned the small area, ready for the long thick needle to be thrust into the port. Once the line was connected and tested, the chemo process could commence. It was a long and laborious repetition of events.

For the first three months, I received treatment every three weeks. The cocktail was made up of three distinctive chemos, each taking about an hour with flushing of the line in between. One of the three was so toxic I needed to fill my mouth with ice for the duration to protect my mouth from being attacked. If I was lucky, I was sometimes given the preferred option of sucking on icy poles.

In the following three months, I received weekly treatments. It was a relief to only have one chemo this time, but again the ice theme continued. This time my hands were plunged inside ice gloves to protect me from nerve damage to my fingers. I did suffer nerve damage in my fingers and my feet. Thankfully I eventually regained all feeling in both. My heart was regularly tested to ensure it was not being compromised during all my treatment.

As the months passed by, I had a niggling feeling of not wanting to go to the hospital. It wasn't the process of the chemo so much; it was the continuous rhythmical sound of the chemo being pumped into my body that I loathed. It was a constant reminder that I was a cancer patient. It's a sound I can't erase from my mind.

My much-loved hair fell out after the first round; so much for statistics. I reluctantly persisted for another three rounds of the cold cap at the insistence of the nursing staff to help stimulate my hair regrowth.

It was about two weeks after my first treatment when I started to notice pieces of my long black hair had made its way from my head to my desk. I still had a few more days up in Brisbane before returning to Melbourne for Christmas and my second round of treatment. I was too scared to brush it and kept it in a bun. I prayed that it stayed put until I made it home.

When home, I reluctantly stepped into the shower and put my head under the running water; it was long overdue to be washed. As I ran my hands through it, it fell away in big clumps. I gathered it all up in one big pile. I hesitantly looked in the mirror at my new minimal look – patchy with random strands hanging on; it wasn't long before they too, ended up on the floor. Again, there were no tears; I took a photo of the pile of hair and started to wear a cap to hide my bald head.

I am a person who takes pride in the way I present myself to the world. I like to wear lovely clothes and make an effort with my grooming, especially given I work in the corporate world. I am also the kind of person that notices everyone else's grooming. I can spot if someone's wearing a new shade of lipstick, if they've visited a hairdresser, or if they have lost or gained weight.

Hence, I was paranoid heading into the office wearing a wig and a few extra kilos. Actually, it was absolutely terrifying for me. I had to harness all of my courage and put on my big girl pants that day. Miraculously, I managed to deceive them all with my shorter, lighter new look. The funny thing was people commented on how much better and softer it was, and I should have made the change earlier. My old black hair was too harsh on my face. I was relieved I had gone with the expensive wig!

I'm not sure why people think it's OK to say, 'Oh don't worry, it's only hair, it will grow back,' to someone who has just lost their hair through cancer. I heard those words often, and I wanted to scream and tell them what I thought. I wanted to punch them. I refrained.

I finished my second round of weekly chemo a week early due to the nerve damage I was experiencing. I was grateful it was over; it made me sick, nauseous, I lost my sense of taste, and I was either constipated or running to the bathroom. I was putting on more and more weight and feeling very fatigued. My white cell count was down, and I was self-injecting to boost my immune system. From there, it was radiation.

My Radiation Oncologist was amazing, and I loved having her as part of my team. I moved to Brisbane for two months so I could work during the day and have radiation each evening; the treatment is very precise and technical and needs to be done in the same hospital. It was a strange process. They make a body mould, so you are in the exact same position for each session. No time to be shy as I am lying naked from the waist up again.

Once the mathematical calculations are all locked in (and matched to the tiny tattoo markings they put on your body), you are left alone in the large sterile room with huge machines hovering over your body. Instructions are given over a speaker from another room. I am counted in, hold my breath, and let the lasers do their thing. Prior to radiation, I had to undergo training to hold my breath. This was so my heart would drop down into my chest and not get zapped by the radiation.

I coped incredibly well through these six weeks to the amazement of the staff. But it was not all smooth sailing. In the last week, my breast and armpit were well and truly overcooked, and I required special dressings and creams to combat the pain. I couldn't get one of those medical bras to fit and resorted to my trusty old comfy bras. I was advised not to wear them, but I ignored that advice. Bra-less is not a good look for the office.

Cancer is a very solitary experience. I was resting, sleeping and sitting at home alone most weekends, not wanting anyone to see me; being hairless was not very attractive. The only positive was not having to shave for a year!

Getting ready for work was like a day's work in itself. It took a huge effort to look like I belonged in the corporate office, putting on meticulous makeup and ensuring my wigs (I had three over an 18-month period) looked natural and didn't move.

Thankfully, I worked in an executive area that had a semi-private bathroom which I could easily get to when needed. Sometimes, I would use this space to have time out and be by myself. During the second round of chemo, I got to the stage of being too scared to eat at the office due to the after-effects. It was exhausting on all levels.

During the two years of my cancer journey, I met with a host of individuals, including specialists, doctors, nurses, surgeons, oncologists, hospital staff, wig consultants and exercise physiologists, with some relationships a lot more challenging than others. I recognised how strong and resilient I was.

I questioned, challenged and engaged in robust discussion when I felt it was warranted, although not necessarily welcomed. I was not your typical cancer patient. I was unrelenting in my expectations and assertive and demanding with hospital staff in order to make the process work for me.

I didn't have time to sit around all day waiting, even though the expectation was if you have cancer, you have all the time in the world. I was a working cancer patient with a schedule to meet, flights to catch, a job to do, a house to keep, family dinners to attend, and parents to look after (yep, I was not given any slack from my family and was expected to do my part).

My wonderful Reflexology community set up a roster to provide treatments. I don't know if they knew how grateful and appreciative I was for their kindness and generosity – it helped me on a myriad of levels, and I loved every minute of it. I also have deep gratitude for the support from my amazing friends.

If I had my time again, I wonder if I would have taken a different approach, meet with other surgeons and oncologists, perhaps go through the public system. I would have saved a fortune; cancer is a very expensive illness. I ended up paying for an additional chemo treatment not covered by the system. This was highly recommended by my oncologist, given my diagnosis and came at a cost of $2,000 a pop – I needed four rounds. I also lost out on recouping the money from my cancelled Central American holiday. Even though I had taken out insurance prior to any diagnosis, it all came down to a 'pre-existing' lump, so another $12,000 was added to the list, along with the cost for surgeries, scans, wigs and regular appointments. I could have put a deposit down for another house!

I didn't take any time off work during the two years, probably to my own detriment. People perceived me to be strong and capable, but that's the billboard that I put on show. Nobody really understood how hard it was to put on a brave face day after day, while all my body wanted to do was retreat and rest.

I did manage to have a sneaky getaway after radiation treatment. I wanted to get away from the grind and embarked on a three-week intrepid holiday to Tibet, Nepal, India and Bhutan, unbeknown to my oncologist.

In hindsight, it was probably not the best destination for someone with a compromised immune system and suffering from fatigue, but I was determined to go and visited the residence of His Holiness, the Dalai Lama Temple, situated high up in the hills of Dharamsala, India to be part of his yearly teachings, and trekked up to the infamous Tigers Nest monastery, perched on top of a mountainous outcrop above the Paro Valley in Bhutan. The trek nearly killed me - what was I thinking!

Although I was used to keeping my own company, cancer gave me the opportunity to have even more time with myself, time to reflect and consider what is important, to re-evaluate friendships, to contemplate who I wanted to keep in my life and who I wanted to let go after their shortcomings had been exposed.

It made me tap into my emotions on a much deeper level. I felt wounded by the lack of support from those I thought would be there for me, and on the other hand, I was joyously surprised by the generosity and care I received from others. It made me slow down and be present, a trait I am trying to, although not always successfully, continue to practice in my everyday life.

It's now over three years since I completed treatment, and I am only now starting to feel like my old self. I do feel anxious when my check-ups come around each year, but so far, so good. I hooked up with a personal trainer to get strong and get rid of the extra 20 kilos – I was becoming a serious contender for the next season of the Biggest Loser!

I wouldn't go as far as to say that this journey has been a gift, but it has given me some valuable lessons and reminded me how powerful the mind can be.

I don't think we are really aware of our limits until we are forced to explore them and find out how resilient and adaptable we can be when we need to. It's helped set me up to deal with isolation during Covid.

I'm making the most of having more me time again, being in the moment, practising gratitude, seizing opportunities, putting effort into my own self-care, expanding my self-development and most important of all, putting myself first.

Adventure After 50

Heather Thorne

Yesterday is history, tomorrow is a mystery, today is a gift - that's why it's called the present.

Eleanor Roosevelt

The memory of the day I left Perth to start my new life in Melbourne is as vivid today as the event itself.

The day started very early. My sister and brother-in-law were taking me to Perth airport for my 6.00 am flight. I'm sure I didn't sleep a wink all night – much too excited. This day was the culmination of weeks of planning, packing, sorting and farewells. Moving to Melbourne had been my dream for several years, and now it was coming true. We had a coffee while we waited for my boarding call. As soon as my flight was announced, my sister, who had been so supportive of my decision, couldn't hold back her tears. Of course, I cried too as I hugged her tightly.

'You're leaving me behind,' she sobbed.

It was just the two of us now in our family of origin, and we had always been close. Mum died the year before, and our father died when we were children. We hadn't talked about her feelings about our separation and, as I write this, I am painfully aware that I didn't ask her. I was too caught up in my plans and anticipating my big move.

Several hours later, I arrived in Melbourne. I nearly had to pinch myself to realise I was really here to live, not just for a holiday. I texted my sister to let her know I'd arrived safely then caught the Skybus into the city. My older daughter, Haley, met me at Southern Cross railway station.

'Sorry I'm late. I couldn't find a carpark.'

She hugged me and burst into tears. Two members of my family crying on me in one day was a first. Tears dried, we enjoyed a light lunch before Haley took me to the serviced apartment in St Kilda, which was to be my base for the next two weeks.

I first started to think about moving to Melbourne when visiting my younger daughter, Marina, who was studying at the University of Melbourne and living on campus at Ormond College. I used to stay near the city centre, walk everywhere and catch trams. We don't have trams in Perth, so that was a novelty. I always felt safe, even walking along Swanston Street at night. While she was studying, I explored the city and delighted in the many attractions Melbourne had to offer. The seed was planted and grew every time I visited.

My older daughter, Haley, followed her sister to Melbourne in 2016. Now, both of them were in Melbourne, and I was in Perth.

I was proud of them for following their dreams, moving interstate to study and build their careers. While I had missed them being close and being able to meet for coffees or a meal, I had no intention of living in their pockets and relying on them for my social life. Marina would not have stood for it anyway. She has always been very independent. No, I was determined to stand on my own two feet, make my own life and further my career.

My last year in Perth was stressful. On Easter Sunday, 2017, Mum died after living for fifteen years with Alzheimer's disease, the last eleven in residential aged care. On top of grieving my loss, adjusting to life without visiting her several times a week in the nursing home and working part-time, I cared for a dear friend who was terminally ill.

Barb and I met at a dementia carer's support group in 2004 and quickly became friends. She was diagnosed with end-stage liver disease in January 2017, and the last year of her life was full of physical, emotional and spiritual suffering. She wasn't an easy person to care for at times, and it was very challenging witnessing her rapid physical and cognitive decline. As the year progressed and Barb's health deteriorated, I helped in any way I could. I remember my sister telling me,

"You're doing too much for her! Where's Jim? He's taking advantage of you."

Jim was Barb's ex-husband, but they weren't divorced, and were still in contact.

On reflection, I don't know how I did it as well as working part-time. When Barb died, I knew that there was nothing more I could have done for her. I still miss her, and the way she was when I first knew her. She was Irish and had the gift of the gab, an amazing storyteller.

Through caring for Barb, I realised how short life is and how precious. She was only sixty-four when she died, and her quality of life in that last year was very poor. My motto became, 'Life's too short for this shit!' I didn't want to die with regrets. I decided that whenever my life was over, I refused to have regrets, refused to think, 'I was going to move to Melbourne, but I never did.'

I hadn't been happy in my job with a not-for-profit organisation for a long time, but with everything going on in my personal life, I hadn't made any serious efforts to find another job. The event that led to my resignation and precipitated my move to Melbourne seemingly came out of the blue one afternoon.

'Heather, can I see you in my office now?' my manager asked.

Going into the meeting, I felt confident about my work, especially the successful event I had conducted that morning. I certainly wasn't expecting to be hauled over the coals. I felt humiliated. Afterwards, I went into the kitchen to make a cup of tea. I felt like one of those cartoon characters with steam coming out of their ears. I was hurt, frustrated and fed up. It was a dysfunctional workplace, and the organisation had changed a great deal in the time I had worked there.

That evening, I wrote my resignation letter.

I knew it was time to move to Melbourne. Sleep eluded me that night as I excitedly visualised myself on the plane on the way to my new life in Melbourne. The following morning, I handed in my resignation and felt a tremendous weight had lifted off my shoulders. I was proud that I had stood up for myself, my values and what I wanted in life.

From resigning my job to getting on the plane to Melbourne was about one month. I found the energy to pack up the unit I was renting, advertise and sell furniture, make numerous trips to the Save the Children store and make plans for the first weeks of living in Melbourne. It was hectic, but everything fell into place. I even sold my car in the last few days.

One week after leaving work, it was all sorted, and I handed back the keys to my rental home I had lived in for the five years since I left my marriage. My sister and brother-in-law kindly hosted a farewell party for me at their home, and we all spent a lovely afternoon eating, laughing and reminiscing with friends.

My first two weeks in Melbourne were spent in a serviced apartment in St. Kilda. Little did I know that I would meet my new partner for the first time at St. Kilda beach eight months later. I took the number 96 tram into the city so often that I could recite the order of stops from memory. Useless information in the greater scheme of things, but it was fun at the time. My first priority was to find a place to live.

Prior to leaving Perth, I decided that I wanted an active lifestyle, that I'd use public transport and walk wherever possible in the course of my day-to-day life. My younger daughter, Marina, was my inspiration in this regard. At the time, she lived in North Melbourne and walked to and from work in Docklands every day. It would take her 30 minutes each way, and as a result of all that walking, she was very fit. Besides, I had always enjoyed doing a lot of walking while in Melbourne on holidays. Perth is a very car-dependent city, and I was used to driving everywhere, so the decision to go car-less was a major one.

I had a mental list of what I was looking for – a suburb with good public transport access, easy walking access to shops and services, and a one-bedroom apartment or unit. Marina came with me one Saturday, and we looked at several apartments as she knew which suburbs would fit the bill. After a few days, I found a modern, one-bedroom apartment in Kensington, an inner-city suburb.

Funnily enough, my older daughter Haley had rented in Kensington briefly before moving to Canberra. When I visited her there once, I had no idea that I would live in the very same suburb and walk past her old place often on the way to the shops. The apartment I found was opposite a large park, and there was a recreation centre across the road. Shops and cafes were an easy five-minute walk, and public transport was on my doorstep. Luckily, I had a five-year rental history in Perth, and a glowing reference from my former agent helped secure the apartment.

I came to Melbourne with two suitcases of clothes and personal belongings, so I had to set myself up from scratch. Shopping trips filled my days. A funny thing happened when I went to buy a bed. Growing up in Perth, it was usually the case that items like furniture, floor coverings, or spare parts for cars had to be transported from 'the Eastern States'. In our family, we always joked that anything from 'the Eastern States' would come on the slowest form of transport available, namely on a camel's back.

Of course, in the twentieth century, even Western Australia has moved beyond camels as a means of transport. Still, it highlighted the physical isolation of Perth from the major east coast cities. So, with that thinking in my mind, I went into a bed shop and naively expected to be able to have the bed I chose delivered the next day. Oh no, the one I wanted had to come from Queensland and would take two weeks. Maybe camel transport was still in use, after all.

Gradually, the apartment started to feel like a home. Fortunately, a friend of my younger daughter was returning to France at the same time, so I was able to buy her fridge, some basic kitchen equipment, crockery, cutlery and wine glasses. I bought flat-pack furniture and hired a local handyman to assemble it. I know my limits, and assembling furniture is definitely one of them.

The whole process of setting up was fun and exciting, choosing what I wanted. I was setting up a house by myself for the second time since my divorce, and I was doing it the way I wanted.

With my accommodation sorted, the next task was to find a job. While I did not expect to land the first job I applied for, I believed my qualifications and experience would be sought after by potential employers. I had two Bachelors' degrees in Education and Preventive Health (Health Promotion) as well as six years of employment in the not-for-profit sector in Perth.

Looking back, I realise I knew nothing about the Melbourne job market, but that wasn't something I could learn about in Perth. The other factor I had not taken into account was ageism. As I was already over 50 when I started my last job, it never crossed my mind that my age could go against me. This took me by surprise.

I was relying on getting a job as a way of meeting people in Melbourne and building my professional network. It was discouraging, to say the least, to be told, 'Thanks but no thanks,' if I even received any response to my application. This was turning out to be harder than I had expected, but initially, I was not overly concerned as I had some savings.

I was also enjoying the freedom from responsibilities for the first time in many years, but there were some negatives associated with that. When you cannot get work, you realise how much it matters in your life, at least I did. I missed the routine, sense of shared purpose with colleagues and mentally challenging work to stimulate me. I was becoming increasingly isolated, applying for jobs in my apartment or the local library.

At that time, I didn't know anyone in the neighbourhood I could have a coffee with or go for a walk. I did attend classes at the gym over the road and stayed on for the socialising afterwards, but I didn't make friends there.

I felt like I had come to a different country, not just another Australian city. Relocating in your late fifties is very different from doing so as a teenager as my younger daughter had done. It's said that you don't appreciate what you have until it's gone, and I certainly agree with that sentiment.

All my professional and social connections were in Perth. Although I am an outgoing person who can talk to anyone, it was much harder than I had expected. I came to Melbourne knowing I had to be proactive about meeting people and decided to join Meetup groups to build a social network. I didn't waste any time putting my plan into action.

The first Meetup I attended while still living in St. Kilda. It was run by a woman, a Career Development Consultant who had moved to Melbourne from Adelaide twenty years ago. At one point, she said something I have never forgotten and often shared with others who have moved to Melbourne,

'When you move, you lose your family, friends and professional connections all at once. It's a lot of loss.'

I had never considered this before leaving Perth. Maybe that was because I have always been able to make friends easily.

Another group I joined introduced me to women who were interested, like me, in attending cultural events such as museums and film festivals. I enjoyed the events I attended with these women but didn't see any of them between meetings. It took until Christmas Eve, nearly six months after I moved into Kensington, to meet a local woman at a book club. Like me, she had recently moved to Melbourne.

After about four months by myself with no job, living by myself and seeing my savings dwindle, I hit a metaphorical wall. I remember telling my sister, 'This wasn't what I thought living in Melbourne was going to be like!'

One Sunday, sick of being cooped up inside, I took the train into the city. Walking up Swanston Street, I was overcome by feelings of loneliness and started to cry. Tears rolled down my cheeks. Desperate to hear a friendly voice, I rang a friend in Perth and blurted out how I was feeling, 'Jenny, I feel so lonely!'

On Boxing Day, my daughters and their partners left to visit their father's family in South Australia. I went to a movie by myself. If I had had the money, I would have gone back to Perth. Maybe it was lucky I didn't – I may not have wanted to come back.

At the beginning of 2019, I joined another Meetup group for women over fifty. I met some lovely women at coffee, brunch and lunches, some of whom became friends. This group allowed me to feel socially connected again, and I eagerly looked forward to events.

On January 13th 2019, I met the man who has a special place in my heart. I knew on the day I met him for the first time outside Luna Park at St. Kilda beach that this was the start of something special. We had met a few days earlier on a dating site, and I agreed to meet him for coffee. From the moment we met, we felt comfortable with each other and spent hours walking on the beach, discovering shared interests, likes and dislikes. That was two years ago, and we're still going strong.

A few months into our relationship, I realised that I had finally met my Paul. Let me explain. My sister is married to a man named Paul, who is kind, caring and treats her wonderfully. I often said to myself that I wanted a 'Paul', a man who would treat me with love and respect as he did my sister. I didn't expect that his name would also be Paul.

Looking back over the last three years since moving to Melbourne, life has certainly been an adventure! It hasn't all been smooth sailing but, even at my lowest point, I didn't consider returning to Perth. Melbourne is my home now.

People ask me if I miss Perth, and I can honestly say that while I miss my sister, brother-in-law and friends, I don't miss the city itself. Mind you, on cold, wintry days, I do miss Perth's more moderate weather. This adventure has made me grow as a woman. Having the courage to move cities at 57 and follow my dream has given me a strong belief in myself. I found a city I love and a man I love. I am now confident that I can achieve any goal I set myself.

Wings of Wonder; My Lessons of Journey

Diane Psaila

The revelation was like a torch in the midst of the night, a guiding light to elation and the result, a heightened sense of empowerment; a conviction that this is what self-respect feels like - a right of path to be the best version of yourself.

Diane Psaila

Moments of Impact, my spirit defined, and apple and almond cake.

I take my seat on the plane. Finally, some solitude after a hectic day. It's early 2021. I feel privileged that I can travel, even if it is only for a short trip. Yawning, I feel my body relax. I flick through a magazine and come across an interesting article on the concepts of critical thinking. It is informative reading that delves into applying the mental processes of analysis, synthesis and evaluation to develop intellectual skills and attitudes in promoting authentic and inclusive growth.

I put the magazine aside and close my eyes. My thoughts slowly drift, like a slideshow, darting in and out, glimpsing the incredible places that I had visited abroad in recent years. I am in awe of the magnificent landscapes and architecture, both ancient and modern, people's culture and their proud, passionate vigour.

I think back to the beginning of 2020, resolutions to renew, a greater focus on health, travel, upskilling and career development. I recall looking on with pride as the last of my three children flew the nest, and like her brothers, set on pursuing goals to build a life of her own. So, there it is, my time now to work on bringing passionate ambitions to a consistent fore.

The year 2020 though, had other plans. It met with the devastating impacts of the bushfires in Australia, and then came the deadly COVID-19 coronavirus pandemic. Evil spreading around the world like an invisible wildfire, with millions falling sick and deaths surpassing three million. Its stronghold had stopped the world's function in its tracks resulting in the economy suffering a hefty battering that will take years to resurrect.

'I can't see you. You are a lethal and contagious enemy. To fight you and survive, I must protect myself by going into involuntary hibernation in my home.'

My freedom was snatched away.
The freedom to visit family and friends.
The freedom to provide essentials and care for my parents without first applying for a permit.
The freedom to shop and dine at my favourite places.
The freedom to go to my workplace.
The freedom to travel.
That normalcy became a distant memory.

Two friends buried their mothers with ten mourners present.
Many others were prohibited from visiting nursing homes.
My son was to be best man; the wedding was postponed.

Isolation at home was my new norm. A venture out in Melbourne's stage 4 lockdown meant a 5km radius limit adorned with a face mask to exercise for an hour or pick-up essentials while maintaining a 1.5m physical distance.

But I know I was one of the lucky ones.
We were safe.
The heroes were the frontline workers who treated the sick and dying. The essential workers who continued with their duties to service our needs.

Home was warm and comfortable.
I could work remotely.
Teachers conducted their virtual classes, and learning continued.
The will to communicate saw creativity and innovation at their best.
The pace slowed; we didn't need to make time. We had time.

People were kinder.
The little things became the big things.
I was given a brown paper bag labelled in decorative handwriting. In it were bay leaves whose hinted fragrance reminded me of childhood and Mum's delicious bolognaise salsa and rabbit stew.

I found a parcel in the letterbox. Facemasks gifted by a neighbour I met during that time.

Community took on a whole new meaning.

Bartering and free giving systems became trendy; circulating homegrown produce and other goods left at the front of homes for contactless collection.

Teddy bears displayed in windows provided a hunt activity for children while they walked with parents for the permitted hour of exercise.

Neighbours came together for the Anzac Day dawn service, solemnly standing in silence at the end of their driveways that were lit with the glow of rows of flickering candles and from down the street came the sound of the bugle call.

I took to watching weekly online sewing classes.
I tested recipes I had earmarked months ago.
I enrolled in a diploma course.

I saw the resurgence and healing images of nature from around the world.
I explored climate change.

How the responsibility lies with each individual to then collectively commit to reducing their carbon footprint for the preservation of environment and planet for future generations.

Social media took on a prominence, becoming a lifeline to connect with family over lunches and afternoon teas and celebrate special occasions from our respective homes. Friends caught up over drinks and nibbles that became a themed ritual bringing home familiar faces, welcoming chatter and laughter.

Colleagues eagerly looked forward each Wednesday to a virtual morning tea break supporting each other with optimism and fun too, with our chic dress dates and status report of the dire state of our hair.

Just as listening to music can elevate mood and stimulate the production of the hormone dopamine, quiet times in my home and garden offered opportunity for meditation; each diversely tantalising the dimensions of mind, body and spirit. Messages of wisdom, hope, energy and love billow, abundant, like the warmth of the sun's rays after a period of grey.

2020 forced a pivotal point in time. Its magnitude imprinted a reality on what's important; of life's fragility and dependency on our natural environment for survival.

~~~~

My thoughts are startled by the sound of a trolley being pushed past, and in the background, I can hear a quiet mesmerising hum. The descent slowly continues. Comfortable and discretely yawning again, I feel my ears pop, just noting a woman's friendly voice making an announcement over the loudspeaker.

Falling asleep, I enter a field of dreams. I am in a lift, and coming to a halt, I walk out to a group of waiting, eager faces.

Echoes of 'Here she comes!' can be heard as I leave the lift behind and make my way to the exit.

Questions aimed in my direction appear to be tactfully worded to entice a reply.

Reporter 1: 'Diane! How does it feel to be living your success story?'

Reporter 2: 'What would you say now to those people who shunned you?'

Reporter 3: 'What's next for you?'

My eyes dart around covertly at the reporters' eager faces behind microphones that just stop short of making contact with my face. Even a head movement on my part doesn't break the focus; a magnet to its prize like gulls feeding on bread pieces thrown at the seashore. Every movement is monitored, in suspense and ready to spring into flight for first pickings.

I imagine winning a publication feature interview is a focus in a reporter's competitive world; therefore, an opportunity for a news story might just open doors to bigger profile assignments.

Wasn't that my life not so long ago?

Different compared to a reporter's life; however, there are similarities, an existence of expectancy and lying-in wait for a winning break.

Feelings of deflation come to mind when after years of hard work and proven capability, implied talk of advancement just did not eventuate. The vision to think outside the box was running a parallel with frustration, draining my energy in striving to prove my worth to an audience to whom I had perceived were better than me and controlled my right to ambition.

'Why play mind games like that?' I would ask myself.

It all seems to point to a status of power and greed to stroke self-image, of social and professional circles who mingle to impress their own kind bound by whatever it takes to maintain the upkeep, irrespective of who is being trodden on in the process.

Somehow the plausible justification for their judgement takes precedence before any thoughts of what is morally right comes into play; if indeed, thoughts of morality surface at all. A kind of formidable force that has a set of conditions to be met before acceptance is considered but dangling the carrot, so to speak, just out of reach but close enough to keep up the interest to visualise a dream come true.

The blatant reflection reminds me of how it was before the penny dropped; a revolving door that suddenly came to a halt, exposing a raw and discerning truth; my time and skills were promoting personal agendas other than my own. It was a wake-up call baring the reality that certain behaviours just don't sit right with me, and living as a byproduct is adding fuel to an existence I didn't like.

I shrug my shoulders. The 'awakening' developed into a surprising and interesting twist, an added dimension that softened my judgement. I began to see the web of complexities and barriers fade and, in their place, a deeper clarity emerged.

The deadly losses due to the COVID-19 pandemic, the long periods of uncertainty, isolation and then the hopeful, stepped easing of restrictions has brought about an understanding of preservation, respect and co-existence. Life is a gift, and time is too precious to waste on dwelling on what was or what should have been, rather focus on ways of identifying what is possible and plan an optimistic way forward.

My experience of the pandemic has been a sheltered one in comparison to the horrific stories of physical and psychological sickness, death, poverty and economic loss; however, it has taught me that striped of wealth and status; we are all the same, ordinary and vulnerable.

What is it then, that makes ordinary people extraordinary? It can be many things to many people dependent on circumstances and perceptions, but it begins from within; the core, a spirited will to make a difference and succeed while ideally upholding a legacy of instilled values.

Elaborating further, like any well thought out plan, a nourished spirit stabilises a journey of growth, discovery and finally, an emergence on how you want to live your life. Consider too, the impacts of twists and turns, the people you associate with, even the brief encounters at a point in time that can influence your choices that come next. Decisive actions towards others and your reactions too are a powerful approach in dealing with difficult people or situations and helps to steer that situation into a positive gear.

Threats can lurk, though, of becoming too overly consumed in a mentality of control and self-worth that can lead to a distortion of reality, thus setting you back from living your authentic self. If left unchecked, this mindset will fast become the very adversaries described earlier.

Reporter 1, noticing my shrug, repeats his question when I start to move away, shorter this time and with a greater intensity. 'Your success. The turning points?'

Maybe it is his earnest look, piercing green eyes in his sun-bronzed weathered face that beckons my attention, or perhaps I recognise something raw in him. An element of me. This is more than just a story. This is seeking advice. I settle in, prepared, yet open to learning. Beneath the layers surfaces a personal appeal, 'I'm stuck in a rut. What's your take on a way out?'

I look at him directly, speaking purposely over the sounds of the camera crew, 'A dear friend once asked me, 'Your spirit within, what empowers you?' I needed to reflect for some time before I answered her, for days in fact, when it finally dawned on me that I couldn't give her a straight answer or even know how to answer. Her reply struck a chord. 'Your hesitation and confusion are signs of a disassociation within yourself.'

'It was that focal point in time that was the beginning of my personal success story. I had succumbed to living an existence that was fulfilling in what I had contributed to others, and that was and still holds an enormous sense of pride and satisfaction to know I have a hand in their well-being. 'Is that it though?' I questioned myself, and again, am l stuck in a cycle of appeasing others and working to maintain an upkeep of my environment, continuously putting what I would like to explore aside with a mentality of, 'One day, maybe?'

'My answer is simply to establish a vital connection with yourself. Pinpoint your likes and dislikes and why. Is it realistic to pursue? Is it confidence in your ability that holds you back?

The reasons may just surprise you but pay attention to the deflective thoughts that invade your thinking process.'

Reporter 1 asks, 'Do you refer to your thoughts navigating towards others?'

'Exactly! It's so easy to succumb to the accepted norm and drift through life, but it defies the right to live to our full potential. Reasons can range from a lack of courage or perhaps fear of rejection, ridicule or failure causing a procrastination trap to freeing and nurturing the inner spirit.'

Reporter 2, the youngest looking of the three, with his golden locks and flushed smooth skin, looks from Reporter 1 to me and with enthusiasm joins in the momentum, 'Doesn't it take experiencing knockbacks to challenge yourself to pick up and try again? The people who brushed you off, would be kicking themselves now?'

A vivid image of my public relations manager comes to mind, frowning in annoyance as he cautions about impromptu interviews. The perception of coming across as one who is not easily attainable and permitting only formal interviews creates an air of earned status.

I'm enjoying this interlude, and an opportunity for candid reflection warms the soul and spreads goodwill. It's all relative, and practising what you preach is keeping it real to avoid being pigeon-holed as a 'hypocrite' or 'being out of touch.' It has a sense of liberation about it, a dual effect of sharing insights.

'Good questions. It is indeed an opportunity to learn from setbacks. Just think about it. As young children, we need to master every growth period. Have you witnessed a child learn to crawl and walk? They stumble time and time again until they achieve the ability to find their balance and do things on their own. Shoelaces? The number of times I went over and over teaching each of my children to tie their shoelaces. The proud look on their faces with a successful result was a reflection of what I felt of their achievement.'

'Why do you think the resolve weakens for some as they go through life?'

Reporter 3, long auburn hair tied in a neck bun, immaculately dressed in a cream pants suit complemented with tastefully applied makeup, peers over her designer spectacles and speaks in a tone that matches her attire, 'Somewhere between our natural ability from a young age to work at facing obstacles with the determination to overcome them, some have, during the course of living, felt discouraged or unsupported to achieve their full potential?'

Reporter 1 declares, 'But it's not as cut and dry as that. Yes, generally speaking, parents and guardians are supportive in encouraging growth and setting us up to achieve success, but as we move into adulthood and beyond, the motivation to step up is the individual's responsibility.'

Reporter 2 pushes away a wayward golden lock from his forehead and turns to the other reporters, 'It's not that simple. Realistically, there isn't always a choice on who you need to deal with on a daily basis. It can take just one or two persons to dampen a group vibe and cause morale to be counterproductive. Our viewpoints or recommendations may not be welcomed, no matter how beneficial or logical; therefore, trying too hard to maintain a relationship or lowering our potential to keep in its favour, is frankly a sign to move on. It's quite good to accept that and have the courage to let it go as it frees up valuable time and energy that can be better placed elsewhere.'

Smiling, I'm enjoying the discussion, and it brings home the value of sharing individual beliefs and perceptions. I notice the reporters were facing each other now, and the camera crew adjusted their target focus. I am out of the equation. An onlooker.

Reporter 3, fixated on Reporter 1 with a look of reproach, zealously replies, 'I know it's not a black or white world we live in, and there are many instances where you need to be watching for what makes people tick. It is like a game of chess. You can't assume your moves are a surety because your opponent can come along and snatch away the work you laboured hard for, and circumstances can change in an instant to upset your once perceived perfect world.'

I make a mental note; outward appearances can mask underlying issues. However, at the same time, outward appearances create an image of a persona you want your target audience to interpret. It becomes a necessary ploy; a win-win at times to survive as a guise in a volatile, social or professional environment.

Reporter 1 in defence, 'Hey, I wasn't saying there isn't any credit in what you brought up, and your reply certainly describes many scenarios, especially the more stakeholders who are nipping at your heels. I just want to add that the constant pressure to be at least one step ahead can have its toll on a person, and yes, I can empathise with them if they just go with the flow, feeling they don't have a choice to up the ante.'

Reporter 2 frowning, looks to be summing up the reporters' replies, 'I agree with where you are coming from, but I say protect your drive to keep trying, and if there are roadblocks to where you want to go, then it's time to take another route. It's a bit of a stage show really; the actor auditions, and if successful, he assumes his character role to a gratifying audience. He works hard and is outstanding in his skill, but there's no guarantee he will step up to a lead role. That's ok if he is happy with his lot, but on the other hand, the people who have the power to make decisions that can step up his career aren't going to help him unless it fits in with their casting requirements and budgets.'

Reporter 3 interjects with a tongue and cheek laugh, 'Yes, loyalty, aptitude and job longevity don't guarantee promotion. Of course, individual and team performances are vital to business viability, however, sometimes the methods applied and pressures can be unrealistic and damaging to morale. The younger generation has a tendency to leave a situation and move on if it's not meeting their needs, whereas older generations have greater staying powers even at the risk of demoralisation. It may stem from overall commitment to the organisation, job familiarity and outside obligations that factor in decision making.'

Reporter 2 frowns, 'Wow, deep, that sounds like a bit of a blame game and playing the victim to me because ultimately, it surmounts to a waste of time and skill. I can appreciate that people can be difficult, even weirdly threatened by diligence, but not moving on because you need to look at the big picture, is frankly, a denial of what we covered earlier; limiting your potential because of living in a comfort zone and accommodating outside situations. Therefore, you are conceding acceptance.'

Reporter 3 raises her well-shaped eyebrows and fleetingly looks over at Reporter 1 with a mischievous glint in her ebony eyes before directing her response to Reporter 2, 'Don't hold back! Indeed, your views are thought-provoking and with them in mind, let's look at another comparison I took from the story of the mother's pride in her children's triumph at tying shoelaces. The significance and trademark of a great leader. The wisdom to recognise, nurture and manage each individual's skill set in achieving success, is in turn, to strengthen the team's function and morale, promoting organisational growth as a whole.'

Reporter 1 quickly diverts the conversation to me, 'Described like that, the contrary is counterproductive. What do you do when people impact your opportunity to step up and further, what keeps you going to reach your goals?'

All eyes were on me again, and the camera crew followed suit.

I hear myself take a deep breath and release it slowly. Somewhere in the distance, wafts of hot food and strong coffee hit my nostrils, making my mouth water. It still takes courage to openly talk about my personal journey. Suddenly I feel an adrenalin rush; my heart pounds, and my cheeks flush. It's mine to control though; the levels I am prepared to divulge, and that reminder is calming.

'Let's answer one at a time, but I must say I have enjoyed the animated discussions between the three of you! I'm sure it's a first to have reporters participate actively like this!'

In unison, the journalists throw a passing glance and a quick, amicable grin between them before resuming their focused stance with microphones at the ready.

'Here it is.'

'As a basis, it's important to regularly reset your state of mind. Each morning walk, I reflect and feel blessed that I am here. I draw inspiration from the sights and sounds of nature and think about my influences and passions in life that positively assist me in strengthening convictions.'

'Fulfilling purpose takes on different meanings for each individual. The goal setters have had challenges to overcome; however, they persist and apply strategic planning and risk management controls to gratify their desired outcomes. Adopting that mentality is relative for all at any standing. It takes focus, dedication and hard work to reap the rewards and continued maintenance to re-evaluate and adjust their path if necessary.'

'The inability to accept setbacks can pose a threat to our capacity in productively moving forward. It's like living in a manifestation of stagnate suspense. Instead, look at setbacks as opportunities to reflect, re-evaluate, make adjustments and steer a way forward. Of course, there needs to be a balance between assuming identities, just like the example of the actor's role.'

'Living authentically is a vibration of our true centre that is dependent on our environment, responsibilities and interactions with others. Envision balancing scales that can tip one way or the other influenced by weighty impacts. The weights are the accepted camouflage that you assume and control to nurture and uphold an even poise.'

'Consider this, what type of person are you when confronted with positivity or negativity? Think of your own circle of family, friends and work colleagues. How do they make you feel when you are with them? Do you add to the mood, whether it is positive or negative? Do they genuinely applaud you in your successes and support you in your times of need? Do you do the same with them? What is your thought process? Are you an opportunist or a pessimist or somewhere in-between, and why?'

'They are loaded questions to get you thinking as they did me. It's interesting really, when you look at it objectively. A person who tends to enjoy being a critic is hard to be around, and it's quite draining maintaining the relationship. It's easy to get caught up in it all, and I recall feeling despondent and saying to myself that it's not who I want to be when I was around someone like that. The realisation became a resolution for change, and the choice for action was in my hands.'

'Human nature is a funny thing. Praise or admiration should far outweigh any focus on unwarranted criticisms, but what do we do? We let others' poor behaviour get under our skin and dampen the mood. That mindset is detrimental to our true potential, and it pays to keep in mind the work and time taken to achieve goals, remembering too, those who have supported the journey.'

'Not so long ago, I had likened myself to a sponge, absorbing others' moods and often not expressing what I wanted to share or having the courage to fully pursue my interests. It was plainly obvious to me that some company I kept were openly not that interested in my achievements. Yet I began to be aware that when something wasn't going right for me it was the opposite. Perhaps it is a lashing out of their own perceived inadequacies or insecurities and my experiencing periods of oppression that suited them just fine.'

'I am a bit of a yo-yo; an extrovert and an introvert too. My collaboration with family, friends and colleagues conveys the best and worst parts of my extrovert persona. On the other hand, my introvert space is grounding, consistent and precious for my well-being; a life without inhibitions embodied in the warmth of authentic awareness.'

'I became a people watcher, and what I saw was interesting.'

'Observation of interactive patterns and the unspoken word are quite thought-provoking, and it has aided in understanding human behaviour. An acceptance of uniqueness and the patience to embrace and respect that right. Yet, there is a confidence now on what I am prepared to take on board and for how long if there is negativity or subordination at play. This doesn't mean life is lived like a detached robot; it means that the environment and the people in it can vastly improve our quality of life. Therefore, surrounding yourself with who and what makes you feel good is a vibration of your inner spirit.'

I look towards reporter 2, 'I echo what you pointed out; if individuals continually don't give you the courtesy of their time; to listen, encourage and appreciate your contribution, then it's time to move on. A mutual respect is paramount in upholding dignity and integrity. Just as it feels good to de-clutter the home from items that no longer serve you and are taking up valuable space, navigate towards those who enhance your inner spirit and limit your time or leave behind dysfunctional relationships.'

'Belief and courage; the basic elements for success. It feels good to say that out loud.'

'Before long, that inner spirit that drives you? You will want to share it with the world.'

Reporter 1 has an air of confidence about him now. 'Is that your vocation in life nowadays? To advocate for others?'

'Yes, starting off with paying attention when people point out your qualities and suggest developing them to see where it leads. People like that are precious gems. I recall way back in 2000 when my life was at a crossroad between letting go of recent disappointments and the courage to push on with added responsibilities and test the waters beyond my comfort zone.'

'Teamed with a passion for communications and process management, creative outlets such as showcasing writing and design were re-surfacing too. A friend who came into my life at that time said, "If you could bottle what you have and sell it, you would be one rich lady." With a dismissive wave, I had laughed at his embarrassing compliment, but I have never forgotten it, and I'm not rich, not in the monetary sense anyway!'

Reporter 2 seemingly thinking out loud, 'Sometimes you need a loyal mate to tell you what you can't see for yourself. It works as a positive plug, and on the flip side, constructive criticism is handy too if you are approaching something the wrong way or investing too much time in a person or situation that you can't change or get anywhere with anyway.'

'Precisely. To improve our outlook on life, where it can take us and how to get there, we first need to acknowledge our imperfections; they are unique to us. Mind they don't override though, as they can deny the right to success.'

'Recently, a friend proclaimed that she is a risk-taker, and when opportunity knocks, she jumps at the chance. This integral belief in capability has served her well. Many would argue that calculated risks are a safer option than acting impulsively; however, it demonstrates our uniqueness as individuals and the ability for transformation by variable means.'

'My journey is filled with a sense of wisdom and pride. The lessons provide the timely ingredients I need for today in keeping my world centred and envision an ambitious legacy tomorrow. I am the author of my journey, a heightened web of experiences and reflections, written to resonate with readers and essentially, as a reminder for me too.'

~~~~

'Excuse me, ma'am?'

'Apple and almond cake with coffee?'

Bewildered, blinking, I direct my focus to a smiling, kind face leaning towards me.

'You were sleeping so soundly and missed lunch. We touch down in Melbourne in thirty minutes.'

Smiling, stretching and nodding in return, I'm feeling invigorated for the next part of my journey.

The power of the subconscious mind is one to embrace; its internal dialogue and depths of the journey is a masterpiece of ingenuity at play. With steely intensity, it is capable of colliding with the conscious world like a jolt of enlightenment, offering its manifest of aura and insights.

I recall in August 2020, in the middle of Melbourne's stage 4 lockdown, Christine Courtenay, widow of renowned author, Bryce Courtenay (d2012), posted a question to followers on social media:

'Do you have a favourite quote from Bryce? I believe some of the phrases he penned are destined to stay with us forever.'

'The Power of One is above all things, the power to believe in yourself" A quote I have recited at every morning walk just when I reach the top of the highest hill. It never loses its magic –

It's been 20 years now! I was at a crossroad at that time. A workmate handed me his copy of the book to read. I have never looked back.'

'Diane, this is so extraordinary, and I just ache to think how much Bryce would have loved to read this too. Thank you so much, and may the inspiration continue to light your way.

Christine x.'

I was filled with warmth, gratitude and a heightened sense of resolution upon receiving that feedback.

Moments of impact in life are opportunities to acknowledge fragility, healing, triumph and enlightenment. The wisdom gained is empowering.

The aroma hits my nostrils - black coffee, warm apple and roasted almonds. I take a bite. Delicious.

Anticipation meeting expectation.
Ordinary becoming extraordinary.
If we let it, the possibilities are endless.

Dedication:
For my beloved children; David, Jarrod and Cassandra.
Dream big. Love Mum xo

Weight Off My Shoulders

Caterina Zanca

The less you see of me, the more of me you actually see.

Caterina Zanca

Hey, fatso!

Here comes fatty boomba!

You have two bums.

You're fat!

These were the harsh words and names I would get called in primary school, just because I was overweight.

As my parents moved a lot with their fruit business, so did I with schools. It was awful always being new, overweight and friendless. I would purposely stay away on school photo days. As a result, I do not have many photos of me at primary school.

Every morning I would wipe away the tears from my eyes, as I struggled to fit into my school uniform. The material would not go over my head. Forget about doing up the zipper.

I always felt envious of girls who could fit into their uniforms. The sad thing was that my uniform was the largest size available in the shops. In one photo of me in Grade 5, you could pick me out straight away. Not only was I overweight, but I was the only one who wasn't wearing a uniform. Why? Because they didn't make a uniform in my size.

My mother would see how distraught I would become, so she asked my aunty to make me dresses to wear at school. Once again, I was the odd one out in the photos as my dress did not match the other students' uniforms. I don't know why my aunty only made green or brown dresses. My father was tight with money, and I seldom had new clothes. Some girls would wear tunics so my aunt made me a tunic, but once again, my tunic was not like the tunics the other girls wore.

I used my humour to try and make friends. I had spent my days alone at home watching comedy shows like *Get Smart* and *Gilligan's Island*. My idol was an American comedian, Jerry Lewis. Comedy was my way to escape and take my mind off my problems. So I became the class clown, and I succeeded in making people laugh. That way, they hopefully wouldn't comment about my weight, and I could make some friends. I still use humour with my friends now, but it is not to deflect from my emotions, but rather, to make people happy.

As an overweight person, my already worsening self-image took another knock at 16 when I did work experience in a Library. The Librarian had to write a report about me for my school. My report stated, 'Her appearance has room for improvement.' I was gutted.

My Physical Education reports made me like feel I didn't belong in those classes. The teachers used to write that I did not participate in sports, which made me feel lazy. I was penalised because of my weight; therefore I was getting close to Fail on my reports.

I was overweight, yes, so why did the school expect me to do gymnastics? How could I walk on those long beams, do somersaults, perform cartwheels, or jump over the pommel horse? The only thing I was good at was rounders and Newcombe, which was like volley ball. I could not even run around the oval or jump hurdles when we were expected to.

My family wanted to help me, and this was shown in different ways. However, none of it was helpful, and often it had quite the opposite effect.

Dad only occasionally mentioned I was overweight. Mum was always understanding and never hassled me. On shopping trips to the supermarket, my mother would make me walk behind the trolley, as I was embarrassed that people would look at me.

When I got home after school, Mum would always have a special treat for me on the couch. Perhaps she knew that I would've had a terrible day and wanted to make me happy, so she gave me my comfort food - a packet of Twisties, or chocolate.

So much for healthy eating, it's almost a joke that I was living behind a fruit shop and would seldom reach out for any fruit.

Mum would do anything to make me happy, and she gave in to my demands, but it didn't help me. If I had the right education when I was a child concerning how to eat well, maybe I could have managed to be a healthier weight. If I only knew then what I know now about healthy eating, I could have saved myself a lot of emotional and psychological pain.

Growing up, I was always compared to my cousin, who was thin and wore much nicer clothes than me. My aunty even gave me scales as a birthday or Christmas present once, and from then on whenever she visited, she would ask, 'Are you using my scales to weigh yourself? How much do you weigh?' I know that was her way of trying to help me, but it didn't work. I always thought that this was really bizarre as my aunt (the one who made my dresses) was bigger than me.

My brother also teased me about my weight. I can still hear his harsh words, 'You will never get a boyfriend or find a job. You're too fat!' I realise now that he probably meant well, but he didn't go about it the right way. Instead of being authoritative, I felt he should have sat down and gently discussed with me the steps I should take to lose weight. Encouragement would have helped. Shock tactics never worked on me.

So my parent's way of helping was to search for a medical solution.

When I was about 11, the doctor put me on the appetite suppressant, Duromine. It didn't really help, so I stopped it soon after.

My world changed when I was 19. We moved again, and I became depressed, spiralling downwards. I found it difficult coping with the move and losing contact with friends and everything that was familiar.

The only thing that saved me was finally finding a job at the Road Traffic Authority where I was not judged for my weight in the interview. I got the job on merit as I had gone to Business College the previous year and I had the clerical skills that they were looking for.

I fit in well at work, and I loved the people. I made lots of friends. Things were looking up.

The answer to my weight loss dreams was across the road. *Gloria Marshall*, a weight loss program, and Duromine again. If only I knew that it would be just the start of my yo-yo weight loss and gain, which was to go on for years. I diligently went to *Gloria Marshall* every lunchtime. I lost over 40 kilos and loved how I was feeling and the way I looked.

The Duromine however, played havoc on my brain and thought processes. I had thoughts of self-harm, and I failed at two attempts on my life. I was put on anti-depressants, but they made me feel worse. I finally found a tablet that agreed with me, so I stayed on that for a while as it stabilised my mood.

We moved away again in 1988. I slowly put the weight back on due to many reasons but mostly because I let myself slip again. I felt like every time I was happy, and things were going well, something would happen to change all that again.

I found a good doctor, and he gave me some suggestions on how to maintain my weight. I bought exercise equipment and tried to do that regularly. The following three years were a blur.

I had put on 60 kilos by 1991, and I had no success at finding any sort of work. Nobody wanted to hire a fat receptionist. My father came with me to an interview once, and he urged the employer to hire me. He pleaded with the employer to give me a chance. I didn't get the job.

I had to do something about my weight. I couldn't find a boyfriend or a job, so I became depressed. I also didn't have a car yet. I felt trapped – physically and emotionally.

I welcomed *Jenny Craig*, another weight loss program, into my life that year, and I had instant weight loss success. I lost all the weight that I had put on.

Things were looking up again. I bought my first car; the boyfriend also came along, then a job in 1992, due to letter drop-offs at places I was interested in working at. I was a receptionist for a physiotherapist, and I was thin. It was okay for a short time, but I became unhappy after a while as many of the clients made unwanted passes at me, even the older married men. I almost felt afraid for my safety. How ironic that all I ever wanted was to be attractive to men and now that I had it, I didn't want it from them.

My relationship was breaking down slowly by the end of 1993, and it was over on Valentine's Day 1994 when I found out that he had cheated on me. I lost more weight without trying, as I was upset and angry.

A couple of months later, I met somebody special through a singles magazine. I hadn't had much success at dating until I met my future husband. I got a marriage proposal not long after meeting him, which inspired me to maintain my weight to fit into my wedding dress.

It was a life-changing time. I felt very beautiful on my wedding day, like a princess. When my brother saw me in my wedding dress, he exclaimed, 'Woooow!'. I could see he never thought I could look so pretty. It felt good that he saw that I wasn't going to be an ugly duckling for the rest of my life.

My wedding photos were something out of a fairy tale. I was so happy that day and found a new respect for myself that I had managed to look thin on my special day. It's what I always wanted since I was a little girl.

My life was fantastic, a little too fantastic, because I put on all of my weight again. My husband had no issue with me being overweight or thin. I had the issue.

In 1997 I went back to *Jenny Craig*. I hated how I looked in holiday videos and photos. I looked so unhealthy, my face was puffy and deep inside, I was sad. Family commented on my weight gain, and my demons gathered again in my head. My childhood traumas had come back to haunt me. I didn't like the fact that people were talking behind my back.

I was inspired again and managed to lose 60 kilos this time. I felt fabulous and could buy nice clothes to replace the size 24 clothes in my wardrobe.

In 1999, I decided to write a brief story about my battle of the bulge and sent it in to *Take 5* magazine. The magazine accepted and published my story. A few days later, they rang me and said a lady from Queensland read my story about my weight struggles. She wanted to meet me, help me and mentor me.

I was so excited to meet her. *Take 5* flew her to Melbourne and she came right to my door, and we got acquainted. We went to the supermarket, and she showed me which foods I should introduce to my diet. She had also struggled for years with her weight and wanted to share her experiences with me.

She told me about the cookbooks she published back in Queensland. She gave me my very own personally signed book. These books focused mainly on how many grams of fat we should eat in a day. The books were great, and helped me understand that I ate too much sugar, and I was eating large portions.

In 2001 I went to Queensland. I had the energy to walk around all the theme parks, whereas in 1996, I had struggled as I was overweight. Back then, I felt so disappointed about how I looked in the videos and photos we'd taken. This time I was so happy that I was not too fat to go on rides. Nobody stared at me as if I was an alien.

As time went on, I realised that I was guilty of judging myself about my weight and how I looked, just as others were judging me. I believe I had so much more to offer, but I could not see that for years. I accepted that I had failed to be myself. I was not interesting enough; I was plain-looking.

At times I felt I was obsessed with how I looked and how much I weighed. I had been conditioned for so long that I must look the part. People used to tell me if your healthy, that's all that matters.

However, dealing with my parents declining health made me turn to food again.

It was my father's death in 2006 when I let myself go again. Then my mother passed away 18mths later. A year later, my husband became ill, and I was his carer for the next nine years of his life until he passed away in 2019. I was busy during those years looking after other people. And my health and weight began to suffer.

In 2017 one of my specialists weighed me, and she said 'Oh my god, Cathy! What are you doing?'

I'm sure she meant my weight. What else could it have been? I must have blushed with embarrassment, and I had no answers for her. I told her and my GP, not to tell me what I weighed each time they weighed me. But in 2018 I asked her. She gave me a record of my weigh-ins, and I saw the figure 122kg from the 2017 weigh-in. I was shocked. I tried the *Lite n Easy* program, but I got bored with the same food and very small portions. I only lost 5 kilos and began eating extra in between.

I began to notice that my feet and legs were becoming very swollen. Every time I went to my local GP, he would not say much. I just wish he told me it was because I was obese. I imagined that I had all sorts of co-morbidities. I began to huff and puff just to go to the letterbox or when I was talking. I could not walk for long or stand up. I was constantly out of breath, but this was also due to my thyroid problems discovered in 2014. I had so many rashes caused by chafing. I did not feel healthy at all. I wasn't happy in any way.

I already had a heart problem from 2008 when my mother passed away. I'm pretty sure it was stress-related and due to me being overweight. I could feel my heart was struggling. I had to do something, but I had already tried numerous times before. This would be another failed attempt.

In 2018 push came to shove. A relative came to visit me and said, 'Gee, you've whacked on the weight!' Well, thank you for reminding me…. again, I thought to myself.

A month later, I was with a friend, and she was telling me about the success she was having with the *Weight Watchers* program. When she told me that she could eat popcorn, ice-cream, and pizza, I was all ears. She had lost some weight, so I thought it must work. She also went for 30min daily walks. She was having so much success.

The next day I signed up for *Weight Watchers*. My last shot, I thought. I was glad to do this program online via digital version of WW. I weighed myself reluctantly – 117kg.

Could I do this? The number was so high. It would mean exercising (ick). Yes, I can do this! I thought of how losing weight could improve some of my health conditions caused by weight gain.

Yes, losing weight was for me, but it was also like an act of secret revenge, showing the bullies that I won't be put down any more. I was proud of my change in appearance.

Some people think we have been 'cured' and feel we no longer struggle with our weight because we lose it. There is no cure. I still need motivation, for if I slip, I can undo all the good I have done since losing my weight.

I've lost 45 kilos in just over a year and a half. Words cannot express how I feel. I'm not used to all the nice compliments I am getting, but I will take them happily. I feel that I'm worthy, as I have changed my outlook on myself, and know that I'm a good person.

I love cooking for myself these days. I make low-fat versions of meals such as stir fry, lasagna, parmagiana, and pizza to name a few. I even make mug muffins for breakfast. So far, I'm maintaining my weight and intend to do this for life. For inspiration, I look at my fat photos, and I'm confident that I'm never going back to being that person again. I want to be forever healthy.

When you feel great and confident about yourself, you radiate that to people around you, and nothing but positiveness can come out of that. There will always be shallow people out there who judge us, but you are the only truthful judge of yourself.

In my opinion, society has played a big part in contributing to some people gaining weight or getting tempted, especially with the chocolates on display next to the check out at supermarkets. Having very thin models and pin-up girls in magazines makes women feel bad about themselves. There are numerous stigmas associated with overweight people. Beliefs and expectations such as; 'you must look thin on your wedding day,' 'you must be a thin receptionist,' and 'men are not interested in overweight women,' don't help either. The list goes on.

A study from the *World Health Organization* stated that Western European people experience 18.7% stigma, and the bigger you were, the higher the percentages.[3]

In 2019, I enrolled in a weight loss and nutrition course. I got my official certificate early this year. I have learnt so much during this course, including that we are conditioned to think we are hungry or need

---

[3] Weight bias and obesity stigma: considerations for the WHO European Region, World Heath Organization, Europe
https://www.euro.who.int/__data/assets/pdf_file/0017/351026/Weight Bias.pdf

food when we don't. We need to break old habits and put in place new ones so our brains can learn a new way of healthy thinking. We also associate TV with snacking. Or when we go out for dinner, we gravitate to foods that are not good for us.

I'd like to now educate and support people with their weight, and also be an advocate weight consultant/adviser. I believe I have personal experience and expertise to help people with anything concerning their weight challenges. I have these skills for myself now.

Sometimes we need a push or a wake-up call to change some aspects of our lives. This can, and often does come from a positive or negative comment someone makes. However, what I have realised is that all along it was up to me to take charge of my life and not rely on what people thought about me. I should have respected myself, I feel, no matter what size I was or how I lived my life.

However, I am grateful for the harsh comments people made. I have turned those negative comments into positive motivation. I found myself ready and in the right headspace and embraced the new changes in me, such as my strengths and improving my lifestyle. I feel reborn again and wish that some of the people from my past could see me now.

The ugly duckling is now a swan.

Where To From Here

Dawn Sulley

Stay true to your dreams. Let your dreams be your inspiration and your guiding light.

Dawn Sulley

I was the fourth child in a family of six. I was adopted out as a three-year-old as my biological parents were unable to look after me and my five siblings. Mum had a misdiagnosed mental illness, and as a result, we were in and out of baby/infant homes, mainly the Church of England home in Melbourne. Dad died in Kyabram in country Victoria when I was three due to a bowel complication.

My grandmother went to visit my mother in Kyabram after Dad's death. There she discovered my youngest brother, who was only four weeks old, hidden underneath a blanket in a bedroom. Mum was too scared to tell the family he had been born in fear he would be taken off her too. With no social security and minimal family support, she found it hard to cope. Consequently, within weeks we were all placed into the Bethany babies' home in Geelong for adoption. My older sister and I were put up for adoption on the condition that we were not to be separated.

We were adopted out to a family in regional Victoria, where we grew up on a beef farm in a tiny town in Gippsland. My brothers were eventually allowed to live with Mum. I have no memory of being in a home or of my parents, or any of my brothers. After being placed in our new home, I grew up believing my adoptive parents were my biological parents and called them Mum and Dad.

I remember when I was around five years old, I was standing in the laundry doorway at home when I told mum that I hear someone calling my name all the time. She looked at me weirdly and said, 'You are adopted.' I asked what that meant, and she said, 'We are not your parents. I am not your mum, and your dad isn't your dad. Your real dad died when you were three years old, and we adopted you and your sister.' Then she added, 'We never wanted you! We wanted your brother Ian and your sister, Linda.'

As a child, I didn't comprehend exactly what was being said. I asked, 'Did my brother die?' Mum answered, 'Why would you say that?' That's when I told her that every night I dreamt of a boy on a train who gets off outside our driveway. She thought I was silly and told me so.

My dream continued on a nightly basis, but I never mentioned it again until I asked to go on a camp and was told I wasn't allowed as my (biological) mum might take me. I cried and asked, 'Who is my mum, and why would she take me?' I went to school and told the teacher in front of the whole class that I wasn't going to camp as my mum might steal me. The teacher asked me to come outside with her and asked what I meant. I tried to explain and she said, 'Don't worry. We will sort something out for you.'

Apparently, the headmaster contacted Mum during the day while I was at school. When I arrived home, I was in big trouble for telling everyone I was adopted. I remember Mum saying, 'Never repeat that to anyone ever again, or I would be put back in the home you came from and you will have to scrub the floor with a toothbrush.'

This threat became a regular declaration in my life, and I felt myself sink into a hole in my mind every time I heard it.

I don't remember my school days and very little of my childhood. Often now something will happen, and a flash will come into my head, and I'll say, 'Oh, I remember when ...' I always felt alone and felt that something was missing. I never felt loved or that I belonged in the family. I can't remember being told I was loved, and I have no memory of being cuddled as a child.

My 14th birthday was a nightmare for me. I was called into the lounge room, and a brown paper bag was thrown towards me along with the words, 'Here bitch!! Just be lucky you got this.'

I opened it through tears rolling down my face and found a black handbag that I was grateful for. I don't remember much after this or the particular reason my sister and I decided to run away.

We planned to leave the following Sunday night after Mum and Dad went to bed. We packed a small bag each and hid them under our beds, along with some money we took from the sale of chicken eggs. After our parents went to bed, we climbed out of our bedroom window, ran as fast as we could up the driveway, and headed into town about 14km away. Every time we heard a car, we dived into the bushes and hid until it was safe. Luckily, we had a torch with us.

We were scared witless of what the consequences might be if we were caught. We knew that it was too late to change our minds, so we kept going. A friend of my sister's had a car, so she rang him from a phone box when we reached the town. He came and picked us up. All I remember was him driving us around until it was daylight. We were undecided about what we would do next so he decided to take us to his mum's place. She must have rung the police as the government welfare team became involved. I was taken to a safe house owned by Berry Street, where I stayed until another family took me in.

My case manager found me a job at the local Target store as a checkout operator. A bank account was set up for me with enough money to live on until I received my first wage. My whole world changed.

My sister decided to go back and live with our mum and dad. I didn't see her again until she came to my work and asked me to go back home. I told her I didn't want to, and that I was happy with my new life, and my new family which included three children. I loved having young children around me. I was often asked to babysit, which I loved as they brought so much joy into my life.

I joined a netball team and played every Saturday afternoon. One Saturday, my sister and her boyfriend came to watch me play. During this game, I happened to sprain my ankle very badly, and they drove me to the hospital. My sister took advantage of this and asked her boyfriend to take her home, where she went inside and told my mum I was in the car. Mum came out and asked me to go inside and said everything would be forgiven in regards to me leaving. I declined the offer, using my ankle as an excuse as I couldn't walk.

After I returned to work a week later, my mum came into work and asked if I would have lunch with her. I said yes, and we renewed our relationship. She was nice to me and would visit my workplace when she was in town.

I decided to change jobs and applied to work at Woolworth's canteen. I loved this work as I earned more money and decided to go it alone. By this time, my sister had left the family home and asked me if I would move into a caravan park with her. It was fun at first until I started seeing a young Italian man who introduced me to a very different cultural experience within his family. I chose to move into a little unit near my work.

I remember the first time I met my mother-in-law to be. She invited me to have a cold drink and asked what I would like. I asked for a coke, and she said, 'Would you like it with some marsala?' I replied, 'That will be nice.' As I took my first mouthful, I realised it was a full glass of straight masala. Trying not to spit out and not laugh, I asked, 'Would you mind if I had some coke in it?' In her full strong Italian voice, she replied, 'You Australian girls are all the same!' She then turned to her son and asked him, 'Why didn't you pick a good Italian girl. Son, you bring shame to the family!!'

Even so, I must have made an impression, as I was invited to my future husband's 21st birthday party, where I met the rest of their family and friends. It seemed unusual for an Italian family however, his dad and younger brother, who was the same age as me, were his only family members in Australia.

We were together for a few months when I became pregnant. His parents insisted we get married. I was only 16, so I had to get permission from the government to get married. It was a whirlwind, and times were difficult because of his parent's resistance to me being Australian. I was blamed for bringing shame on the family by getting pregnant. I had a new culture to learn.

Our first beautiful daughter was born five months into our marriage. The pregnancy wasn't easy. I was diagnosed with pre-eclampsia and spent the last month of my pregnancy in the hospital. The doctor decided, due to my complications and age, that I should have a caesarean.

It was November 1976, and in those days, you had to stay in the hospital for two weeks post-caesarean. After taking my daughter home, I couldn't settle her. She was crying and constantly hungry, so I supplemented her feeding by bottle. Three months after the birth of my first daughter, I found I was pregnant again. My pregnancy wasn't well-received within the family, and nine months later, in the summer of 1978, I had another beautiful daughter by caesarean.

A couple of months later, my sister and I received a letter from a man asking if we were related to the Bennett family, and if this was the case, we were possibly his sisters. We didn't know what or how to feel. I was very excited and couldn't wait to be part of my own family again. After several letters, I finally received a phone call from my eldest brother Ian who explained that we had not one but three more brothers. Ian also gave us bad news; our biological mother had suicided just months earlier. I felt distraught as I never got to meet my mum.

We decided to meet our brothers for Christmas. In another twist, that same evening I received a phone call from a man saying he was my half-brother Laurie. He explained our dad had been married previously, and there were another four children – two boys and two girls. Laurie also told me our Nan was still alive and was very excited and wanted to meet us. We discovered she lived only an hour and a half away.

To think, I had driven past her door almost weekly each summer going to the beach. What other surprises were in store?

Our third baby was born in the spring of 1982, a beautiful boy. I had my tubes fused during his delivery via caesarean. I was 23 years old. All of our children were loved by the family and spoiled with gifts, clothes, food, holidays and never wanted for anything.

Christmas 1990 was the best Christmas. I had my Nan staying with our family, my sister, her family, both sets of parents, and everyone got along for the first time. Our family felt complete. After Christmas, Nan went to stay with her eldest grandson, my half-brother, and his family. This had been a family tradition of Nan's for years.

The New Year came and went Nan returned to her home where she would meet up weekly with her friends at bingo, which gave her so much joy. I received a call one evening from Nan's neighbour saying that Nan had a fall on her way to bingo and had been taken to the hospital where she was waiting for an operation after breaking her hip. I went straight down to see her. Nan spent many weeks in the hospital. After speaking with her doctor, it became obvious that she wouldn't be able to live by herself again.

She was moved into an aged care facility. After visiting her there several times, she told me how much she hated it. Nan told me she might as well die. I witnessed her just sitting in a passageway with about 20 other residents. They were all lined up, sitting in a row with nothing to do until it was mealtime. All their meals were lined up and put on their trays in front of them. After lunch, one by one, they were taken to their rooms for an afternoon rest until dinner time.

They were brought back out at dinner time, then back to their rooms in time for bed.

It was awful. I couldn't sleep as it had affected me badly. I couldn't think of anything else. I said to my husband, 'I can't let this continue.' I had only known my Nan for eight years, and I was lucky to have had the opportunity to spend time getting to know her. She didn't deserve to be treated this way, so I arranged for her to come back to live in our family.

I loved spending time with Nan; she enjoyed a good joke, loved her sport, cricket and footy. Being a one-eyed Collingwood supporter, when the grand final was on, we decorated the lounge in black and white, shared a shandy with her and cheered along with her. Nan was grateful she spent time with us.

Christmas came around quickly, and Nan was invited to spend time at my brother's place. The following day we took Nan back to her home town and stayed with her until family from regional Victoria took her on holiday over the New Year with them. The day we left Nan's, our family went to the beach. I wasn't feeling well, and fell asleep on the beach, not waking up until it was time to leave. The next day we had New Year's lunch at the in-laws. I still wasn't feeling 100% and wanted to go home, but instead of going home, we decided to take the children to the park.

Whilst there, I became very sick and I was in a lot of pain. I was rushed into emergency, where I was diagnosed with an ectopic pregnancy. I nearly died as my ovary and tube had burst, and I was losing blood fast. I had emergency surgery, and when I woke up, I couldn't comprehend what had happened. It took months for me to recover. I was in total disbelief as to how this could happen, but life had to go on with two teenagers and a seven-year-old to care for. Luckily it was the school holidays, so my children went to stay with their grandparents for a couple of weeks.

After I came home from the hospital, I decided I wanted to be near the children and travelled to my parents to be with them until I was able to go back home. Their father continued to work during this time.

After going back home, I had to take things easy. I felt guilty as the school holidays came and went without me spending much time with the children. School holidays finished, and the children went back to school. My brother offered to let Nan stay for a few more weeks; however, when she returned to live with us, it was evident her health had declined.

Nan hadn't been eating well, so I took her to the doctor, who said it was time to put her into care as her health was declining. Within weeks, she passed away. My sister and I were with her when she died. I felt blessed to have been with her at her passing; she looked peaceful with a smile on her face as if someone was there with her. I assumed it was her husband, someone I had never met.

My father-in-law passed away a few years later in 1994, and from then on, our family seemed to fall apart. My eldest daughter moved to Payneville in East Gippsland after meeting a young man. They quickly become engaged and moved in together. Another of my offspring, daughter number two, left home in the same year and moved interstate with some friends she had met through work. I was shattered. I had to move forward as my son needed support starting high school.

Another shock was about to take place on Boxing Day 1994; my daughter's fiancé was killed by a gang of young teenagers. I wanted to be close to her to provide support and guidance, so we decided to move to the seaside town of Paynesville, where my original foster parents lived.

My husband stayed behind working until he found a new job, which took a few years. I don't believe he intended to find work in the area. I felt like I was a single mother looking after my teenage son. I was feeling emotional burnout and was exhausted working three jobs and not getting anywhere. I desperately needed a purpose in life. I was 42, my son was 19, and moving away to be with his girlfriend who was at university. I decided I wanted a stable career, so I decided to return to study.

I studied hard at Tafe. I was proud of my achievement, completing my Diploma as a Diversional Therapist, which opened many doors within the aged care industry. My husband didn't like me studying; my marriage broke down, and my world fell apart.

We had grown apart after 30 years. Due to the nature of the marriage breakdown, my girls stopped all communication with me, my former husband and the rest of the family. I used to look after my granddaughter almost every weekend until she started kinder. I never got to see her after this, and I felt shattered.

My son had just married and moved back to the country. I loved having my son and daughter-in-law in town. I had my mum to confide in, and she supported me. We went on many drives together and enjoyed having a meal out at least once a week. I had to make a new life for myself. I joined the local croquet club and made new friends through work and study.

One Sunday afternoon at the local supermarket, I met up with a friend who suggested I try online dating. I found this very daunting. After talking with many online strangers, a lovely man, Stuart, contacted me.

We became friends and spent many years getting to know each other. Then one day, out of the blue, Stuart proposed in a roundabout way. I was at work; Stuart was sitting with his mum who was living in the aged care facility where I was working. Stuart said to his mum, 'I've known Dawn for a while. She should become a Sulley.' His mum replied, 'I thought you were already married.'

I spent the afternoon replaying his words in my mind. Did he ask me to marry him, or did I misinterpret his words? It wasn't until I started receiving text messages and phone calls congratulating me that it began to sink in that he had indeed proposed.

As I walked down the passageway, I received a call from my son, who asked where I was. I said, 'I'm at work.' He said, 'So you're engaged. I just received a text telling me so.' I replied, 'I must be,' and laughed. Stuart had sent a text to everyone to announce our engagement, so everyone found out together to avoid any issues about who was first to know.

On the following Monday morning, we set about by choosing an engagement ring, but we bought a wedding set as they were on special. We decided to have a short engagement as we wanted to travel. We didn't want a large wedding. Stuart had a big family who made up a lot of the guest list.

By now, my son and daughter-in-law had two beautiful children, a girl and a boy. We enjoyed many family meals and events together. He and his new wife supported me emotionally for a few years until Stuart and I married.

The day after our wedding, we thought we'd have a BBQ and started inviting close friends and family who had travelled to the wedding. I rang my son. He was very strange on the phone and declined our invitation. I didn't think too much of it until a few days later when he came to visit me and told me they decided not to include me in their lives anymore. They could no longer be friends with me as he had reconciled with his sisters.

I was devastated. I could no longer have contact with my biological grandchildren. Thankfully, through my marriage, I had five beautiful grandchildren who regard me as their grandma. After marrying in the winter month of July, we travelled overseas. We travelled through England and France and had a wonderful time catching up with cousins Stuart hadn't seen for years.

After returning from abroad, I decided to further my career and gained a higher recognition within the company I worked for in the aged care sector. I started working towards volunteering coordination. This position allowed me to travel to other facilities and educate lifestyle staff. In my new role, I found my passion for education.

I became a vocational teacher, teaching Certificates 3 & 4 in both aged care and leisure and health. After working for various Registered Training Organisations and in the Tafe sector, I was offered a role in Melbourne.

After much deliberation, we finally decided to make the move. It would involve selling our new home in Bairnsdale. We decided to downsize and bought an apartment in Docklands, Melbourne, in the heart of the City.

I was in my element. There was so much to see and do for free; markets, restaurants, outdoor events every weekend, visits to family and friends we never used to see very much. I decided I needed to widen my friendship group, so I joined a meet-up group called *Radiant Women Over 50*. It was a new group, just finding their feet, and I made many new friends.

In the teaching industry, you need to be working within your field, so I applied for a job at the Alfred Health Caufield Hospital campus. I was so excited to get this position.

I learned a lot working with a fabulous team of doctors, nurses, and other health professionals, overseen by the best Unit Manager ever. Times were good.

After work, we had a great social life, going out to the *Comics Lounge* to see personalities like Tommy Little and Pete Heliar and Nazeen Hassain, to name a few, attending weekend markets and festivals like Moomba, which were free to watch. It was an amazing time.

We were able to spend time with my Uncle, who was unwell and being treated for cancer. After being in Melbourne for five months, I became sick and visited the doctor. After a ten-day course of antibiotics, I was still unwell. I was sent for a scan that showed I had ovarian cancer. Our world changed again.

I went on sick leave, and despite my employer holding my job open for nine months, unfortunately, I had to resign. I finished my treatment and decided I needed to be near our family and friends. Stuart would have been happy to stay in Melbourne a lot longer, but he understood why I felt like I did. I'm forever in his debt now.LOL.

We sold our apartment and bought another home in the country, which we are grateful for now with the corona-virus pandemic in Melbourne. Cancer has forever changed my life. Until a cure is found, I will remain on a maintenance program as long as my body can take the medication I am prescribed.

To finish on a positive note, my son, daughter in law and eldest daughter, along with my grandchildren, came to my 60th Birthday party, which was the highlight of my day. My daughter sent me a Mother's Day message this year, which was lovely:-)

My journey hasn't always been an easy one, but throughout, I have always tried to be true to myself, my values and my beliefs. For that, I am grateful.

I Have A Story To Tell

Francis Borg

*Yesterday I was clever, so I wanted to change the world.
Today I am wise, so I am changing myself.*

Rumi

Journey To Me

As I look back on my life, I realise that every time I thought I was being rejected from something good, I was actually being directed to something better - Steve Maraboli

People regularly ask, 'When and why did you decide to become a relationship therapist?'

My name is Francis Borg, and I am an Imago relationship therapist and couples workshop presenter, and I have a story to tell.

I wasn't always these things, and in fact, I never aspired to be a business owner, therapist or, more specifically, a relationship therapist and couples workshop presenter.

I am passionate about my work, about this theory about self, relationship and connection. Yet there is so much more about this work, this journey of being conscious and taking action (not reaction) in one's life. I am now so passionate about this theory and how much sense and peace I have gained, that I share it will all of my clients. I share with them how things have changed about me, for me and all about me. This theory can be helpful to anyone.

I had regularly described myself as a lifelong learner, and I have a litany of professions, paid or unpaid, in the public or private sector, and certificates and participations I have completed or attended throughout my life.

In 2005, I was completing a Master in Social Science majoring in Pastoral counselling, working as a casual at the Royal Brisbane and Women's Hospital as a midwife and registered Nurse. At the same time, I was working part-time as a probationary support worker at a Women's and Children's refuge not too far from home.

Oh, home - I am married to Ian, and at that time, we had six children, five young adults and teenagers and an 18-month baby. Yeah, what was going on there!!!!!!

At the completion of my 12-week probationary position at the refuge, I was called into the office and told that as I did not fit into the organisation/team, I would not be offered the permanent part-time position I had been working towards at that facility.

It was around then that I started to think and believe about myself that 'I was problematic', 'I did not fit in', and that 'I did not belong'.

It was then that I used the 'F*** word', and I was not saying 'Francis', if you get what I mean. I decided that I was never going to work for anyone else again. I began telling everyone, my husband and family, and anyone else who might have been interested, that upon completion of my Masters, I was going to open my own business as a therapist. And on the 1 September 2006 that is exactly what I had achieved. I launched myself in private practice as a Therapist. I had an office and began advertising and looking for clients.

Of course, I had no idea how to start a business, yet I learned quickly. I also began experiencing ALL of those negative people who just showed up and asked questions like, 'How are you going to do this?', 'What's your business plan?' and 'Where will the clients come from?'

They were ALL good questions, and even after these many years later, I realise how naive I was then. The worst comment came a few days into my new venture, my new practice, when a visitor called in to introduce herself and said, 'You know that most new businesses fail three times before they get up and get going.'. I understood her to be telling me that I was going to fail. So much for well wishes and good luck.

But I did get started; I was a legitimate, legal, a registered entity. I began my business in my name Francis Borg as a Sole Trader, and within a few years, I changed my business name to *Brisbane North Counselling*. I initially promoted myself as a Family Therapist.

My thinking about starting as a family therapist was that I came from a big family. Ian and I have a big family, and I had many experiences in school communities, and sporting clubs with families and since the age of 17 worked in hospitals, training or as a registered nurse and midwife. I completed further training as a family therapist, attended regular training in groups and got a great supervisor (even though at times, I didn't always see eye to eye with her). That relationship did change and flourished with time. And I felt confident enough to get established and get out there.

One powerful message stayed with me from my previous uni days whilst completing my masters. There was a visiting lecturer from America, and it was free to attend his talk. He was a researcher for health funds, and this particular lecture was about what people/clients say about the therapist-client relationship. The message I took away from this event was that his evidence very clearly showed that for a client to feel improved, feel heard and listened to was not about how old, or how clever, or how experienced, or well-read a therapist was. For clients, the important thing was to feel that the therapist was there really there for them. I knew how to do that, and I am that.

Maybe I was lucky, maybe the Gods were with me, maybe the universe was looking out for me, or maybe I really had something to offer, because within the first 12 months, my business was looking good, and by the second year, I had come out even and generated some good business, and the books (meaning my accounts) were looking looked good to me

I was happy, and yet I began developing anxiety, which is never comfortable,full stop. Sometimes it was full-blown, which would look like loss of sleep, overthinking and losing my hair. Upon reflection, it happened because as I focused on my business, I stopped doing all those other things that gave me release and enjoyment, like playing or coaching netball, the lunches or coffee mornings with friends and other school mums and knitting, which I love to do. It took many years to realise that many business people have this same problem.

I continued as a casual midwife at the RBWH and in my Counselling practice, going to training and following the never-ending paper chase of leads and eventual real business.

I enjoyed many aspects of being a small business owner, and I always knew that I was not looking for a full week of client load, nor was I looking to grow my practice to include employees. I always knew that working or managing colleagues, etc., was not my strength. So, I wasn't a business-minded person looking to grow and sell off my business. I proudly called myself a small business and meant it as I was happy with my small quota of weekly clients, which was growing nicely and began showing in my increase of weekly/monthly income. Yes, it was important to me to see measured growth like that also.

A surprising thing started to happen for me quite early in my new career/business - a number of couples became my regular clients. Of course, it was surprising then, and not so surprising NOW. It makes sense as I had been working as a midwife since I was 18 years old, and hence being, talking, and working with couples was familiar and perhaps easy enough for me.

I would hear from other therapists that working with couples or families was not comfortable or even too hard. Please don't get me wrong, there is a lot to take in with each extra person in the room. Yet, I was comfortable, and with time and further training, I got better and even good at working with couples.

Most of the time, I did really good work with couples, and one thing that would show up from time to time was that sometimes couples would become distressed, fight, argue, and get highly reactive. At these times, they sounded worse than my husband and me on our worst days. It was not a good thing to witness.

When this happened, I realised sadly that sometimes these couples could leave my rooms worse than when they came in, and that at these times, I was not in control of what was happening in a session and in my own rooms. That's when I decided I needed further training and specifically 'couples' and 'relationship' training.

So, I began searching for relationship counselling training. At first, it wasn't so easy to find where to go or what to train as (meaning type or theory). Then, when I found the training, I wanted there were new obstacles, in particular, interstate travel and later, even overseas travel.. The training for couples/relationship counselling required being away from family and home and work for days/weeks at a time And importantly, my youngest child, as she was still under five years, so the training went on the back burner until she was older.

In 2012 I began once more seriously searching for training in relationships counselling, and it was Imago Relationship Theory and Training that resonated with me. I suppose what I read about this theory triggered and interested me.

I could not begin to explain or share all that happened the day I began a two-day introduction to this theory in Sydney. What I can share is that I had an experience very early in the training that I liken to waking up, shedding some of the cloud and fog that I lived with. I was being asked questions about myself and finding answers about me.

Until you make the unconscious conscious, IT will direct your life, and you will call it FATE – Carl Jung.

One powerful revelation was that I had negative words and beliefs from childhood to describe myself; beliefs like: I am problematic. I don't belong. I am lonely being part of a big loving family. I am living in a big house, and I feel ALONE. All of these beliefs from my childhood were beliefs I still carried with me into my married life. And I didn't feel good while expressing or living those beliefs. Well, that was then and NOT now.

The other powerful aspect of seeking relationship counselling training that became apparent was that. I thought and said so many times that I was seeking relationship training so that I could be the very best at helping couples and their relationships.

What I realised was that how could I be a great relationship counsellor when there was so much about myself and my relationship that needed to be repaired, understood and healed. It was like sending in a train wreck to fix other train wrecks. 'What was I thinking?' Well, that was just one of the many things. I also began to realise that I was never good at thinking before taking action. (Remember all those good questions I found so negative as I was beginning my business venture).

It is now ten years later, and finding me began during that two-day introduction course, and so much has come to light. Well, now I am ME, happy, I belong, I am connected and loved, and things are good with my husband, even on our worst days. I also now enjoy a good relationship with all my children and grandchildren, mostly. But this is jumping ahead.

After the two days - introduction and training, I realised that this is absolutely the course and experience I wanted. To become an Imago Relationship Therapist, I had to (as do all trained Imago therapist) attend a couples workshop with my husband, and that was something I had never considered. I mean, the very thought of asking Ian to come to counselling with me was unthinkable, and the only word that came to mind was 'NO Way' (two words).

Ian and I had been married for 30 years, and many times he had said that counselling was my stuff. Ian was a construction manager and always drew a line between what I do and what he does. You stay over there, and I stay over here. So how was I going to get Ian to attend a couples workshop?. And with me. That was how I used to think and behave, not so any more; change began from that very day I started Imago training. As an aside, now I have couples and men as clients from every possible profession, trade, area of life, as everyone is an individual. So my generalising about construction workers was incorrect.

There had always been a lot of passive-aggressive behaviours that were part of me. And without blaming anyone, it is what surrounded me in my childhood. I might even say that this is how I knew to communicate my needs which doesn't make it right. Anyway, it had never worked for me as generally until then; I was quite lonely in my marriage. It is how I behaved then.

I had a few discussions with Ian about coming and doing a couple's workshop with me. I had even given him the book *Getting The Love You Want* by Harville Hendrix and Helen La Kelly Hunt, the creators of this *Imago Theory and Therapy*, to read. The couples workshop was based on the work in this book. Ian is an avid reader, and he did read the book and said to me, 'Great book.'

I communicated so well to Ian about us doing this couples workshop together (NOT) that we ended up in New Zealand and at the accommodation, the night before attending the two-day couple's workshop, I overheard Ian sharing with other couples at the accommodation that he was there as his wife (me) was in training to become a relationship therapist and he

(Ian), was needed as her guinea pig, to practice on during the workshop.

Does it sound like he knew he was doing a couple's workshop with me? NO.

Was I cringing, holding my breath in case someone told him or corrected his statement before we got to the workshop? YES.

The next day we made it to the workshop just as it was starting, and with great relief by morning tea when we stepped outside on that very cool, rainy and blowing Auckland day, Ian turned to me and said, 'I get it now; we are doing this couples workshop, and this is very good.' WOW.

Those two workshop training days went so quickly, and I found myself enjoying the written work in the manual provided for each participant (and I wrote so much). The manual work was just for Ian and me to write, read and share with each other the processes that we undertook, and they were easy enough for both of us to achieve.

There were trained therapists who we could call over to help us do the processes but only if we wanted help. There were many insights into my childhood that assisted me to question the old beliefs I had about myself. I now had so much more to start with and believe instead. I had survived and, up to then, really enjoyed an exciting active life and that there were a treasure box and abundance of new words and beliefs to aptly and positively describe ME. I just couldn't see it up till then.

It was upsetting, distressing, insightful, and a huge relief to attend this workshop with Ian. I left shaken by what I now realised about my childhood and what I had misunderstood, misnamed, and missed out on. It would take more time and working with the processes for me to be happier in myself.

So Ian and I flew home, and Ian set up a weekly two hour appointment time for us to sit and use our newly acquired communication skills. No more passive/aggressive assertiveness for me. No more aggressive communication or dismissive behaviours on Ian's part.

We began to practice our new skills; We had been shown so many new ways to be safe, connected and have fun and acknowledged the positive difference between us. So much so that I had a bevy of unexpected and yet wonderful follow-on stories to share about those early days post doing the couple's workshop. You see, our youngest daughter was about eight years old then, and we had our eldest daughter and her husband come and stay in our home with her while we were away.

We didn't tell our older children about attending a couple's workshop. As you have read, I was not even clear to Ian that we were doing a couple's workshop. They understood that I was doing some training in New Zealand, as I had missed the Australian workshop dates due to my commitment to another volunteer event that same weekend. Their dad had told them he was coming to help me as my guinea pig.

One Sunday, around five months after we had returned from the couple's workshop, our elder three children were visiting as usual. I always thought they came to catch up with each other and their dad and not to visit me. This particular Sunday, Ian and I were in our backroom together, and the youngest of the three in her mid-20's was walking around us kind of circling us and asked, 'So what's going on?' 'So, tell us what's happening?' 'Go on what?' I looked at our eldest children with a puzzled expression, unsure what my youngest meant and not sure whether they understood it. I wanted clarification, and all three asked, 'Well, how come you two are in the same room together?' and 'How come you like each other?'

Wow, I got it then. For all their growing years, they had not experienced their parents quietly being together. We were now behaving so differently, too differently, that they started to think that something was going on and they thought or suspected that one of us was terminally sick.

Of course, we assured them that all was well. In fact, it would be some time before I shared with them that Dad and I had attended the couple's workshop and had learnt how to be safe and connected and be loving towards each other.

I suppose what that event highlighted for me was that all those years when they were younger, Ian and I were not very nice to each other or safe in front of them.

They had observed how unhappy and disconnected we were. It still hurts thinking about how we were silent in front of them, fooling no one.

Now all these many years later, we continue talking openly in front of them, including them, speak positively about our days, and we share what we have been up to during our week. This usually includes what we have been doing together as well as individually. And we allow them to come and share their lives with us; they have boundaries just as we have boundaries.

I am happily connected with Ian and all our children, and when a difference or disconnection shows up, we have the skills to discuss and repair our connections. While Ian and I model how we get on, we are modelling to our children and grandchildren how to be safe, stay connected and repair when upsets and ruptures happen. And ruptures and upsets do sometimes still happen; they are just much further apart. Our skills have become second nature, and we are better listeners and ask for more information.

So, in conclusion, Why did I become a relationship therapist and couples workshop presenter? Well, at first, it was by chance that a series of similar events kept happening to me that I had to finally pay attention. It was my chance that ALL roads led me to discover that I needed more information about myself and why I became that person with beliefs of not belonging, of being alone and lonely, until I allowed a safer connection and experienced the positive benefits from attending a couples workshop. It enabled me to address and repair some of my childhood wounds and think more compassionately about my parents. Ian and I were able to address our relationship wounds because we could express more about the childhood pain, and now this generational change was affecting us now. It also enabled me to address the wounding of my children and communicate better with my children and grandchildren.

If I had that first impression that Imago theory would help me in my couple's work, I now grasped that first, it had to help me, my family of origin, my husband and children and grandchildren. Bonus, BONUS, **BONUS.**

So why am I passionate about being a relationship therapist and couples workshop presenter? It is because it absolutely brought about so much positivity for me.

I like me, I love my husband, and I understand the work needed to model being a woman, a partner, a mother and a female in our world. Why wouldn't I want to share it with the world for others to achieve too!

My Money And Lipstick Story

Suze Elford

Train yourself to find beauty in every situation and learn to create your own sunshine.

Suze Elford

Life is not easy for anyone. Life is not always perfect. Most of the time, we cannot control what happens to us. One thing I know for sure, we can control the way we respond to what's happening, and we have the ability to choose how we react to what life throws at us. Everything that's happening in our lives has a story to tell. Somewhere in the story lies a message if we choose to see it. Those messages give us lessons to learn, wisdom to share.

So this is my story - a story of my experiences that I hope will inspire someone. We were all born with a purpose. It is up to us to discover what our purpose is so we can live our life with intention.

> *Life is 10% what happens to you and 90% how you react to it.*
> – Charles Swindoll

On 6th April 2020, I lost my dear mama. I dedicate this story to my Ma – a stunning woman who has given her life to others. She made many sacrifices, putting others' needs before hers. She has shaped me to be the woman I am today. Ma, to the world, you are just a 'mother'. To me, you are my hero, my absolute

WORLD! Your unconditional love, undivided attention, your heartfelt teaching, and mostly your contagious smile and laughter brings me joy as I go on living my journey in this thing called Life. Thank you for choosing me to be your daughter.

I also would like to dedicate this story to the other special woman in my life, my beautiful daughter Sasha Nichole. Sash, you have taught Mummy the meaning of love, loyalty, and to see the beauty in others. Believe in yourself, go after your dreams and keep spreading your wings to shine in everything you do. In your eyes, you think Mummy is your hero. The truth is, you are the gift life has given Mummy. Love you with all my heart, always!

My Mama Always Said

Growing up Mama always said, 'Su, money does not always buy you happiness, but money gives you choices.' She added, 'As a woman, our best protection is a little money of our own.'

Her advice to me was to find a way for financial freedom so I don't have to constantly worry about the 'what ifs' of life. She often reminded me to always be prepared as life is unpredictable. She said, 'You never know what is coming next.' 'Be peaceful, stay contented but don't ever get too comfortable. Be prepared for the unexpected.'

My Ma reminded me, 'Su, no matter what day you're having, and even on the days when you just want to hide from the world, always always wear your lipstick.'

She said, 'There will be days in our lives when the world makes us feel pale, so brighten it up with your favourite lipstick, and with your best foot forward, keep on moving.' 'Be your own hero; the hero is inside you.'

My mama was full of wisdom. I never understood where her positivity and strength came from. She battled with many unkind days. I was too young to understand. But one thing I remember so clearly is how comforting and safe she made me feel when I saw her in her bright red lipstick. Her presence, the energy she carried, made me believe that she could make anything possible!

Now, as I go on my own journey of life, I understood what her message was in her story. How can we pour from an empty cup? How can we give to others when we have nothing to give? How can we love others if we don't learn to take care of ourselves first? How can we live with love if we give hate to the voices?

Life is unpredictable. We don't choose some of the things that happen to us, but we have a choice of how we react to it. So, if a little waxy bit of colour on my lips gives me a great start to a brighter day, why not!

If you want to have enough to give to others, you will need to take care of yourself first.
A tree that refuses water and sunlight for itself, can't bear fruits for others.
–Emily Maroutian

Mirror Mirror On The Wall, Who's The Fairest One of All?

Born in Malaysia, I was the third out of six children. Growing up, I was labelled as having a Middle Child Syndrome. Middle Child Syndrome is the belief that middle children are excluded, ignored, or even outright neglected because of their birth order. And in the culture that I grew up in, I was even more excluded due to my dark colour skin.

It seems silly in this 21st century to hear it and may even be unacceptable but back then in the town where I grew up, if you have a light skin tone, you are perceived as prettier, smarter and more superior and usually are given more privileges. One tended to receive more love and attention from the family if you were born with fair skin.

As a young child, I never understood why some adults found it okay to make anyone, let alone an innocent child, feel that she is inferior, feel different, and feel unworthy. To feel that you are not pretty enough, not good enough, and not smart enough are not great feelings to have growing up. We have no control over how we were born, especially when it comes to race, colour or religion.

Growing up, I avoided family gatherings; I wanted to be invisible. I felt more comfortable and safer being on my own.

After school, I would be playing in my own little corner in my bedroom and sometimes in my tiny backyard with sand and dirt. I remember sitting under the shade by the large bamboo trees in a neighbour's vegetable garden playing make-believe with my imaginary friends. I remember those days where I was just happy being by myself. I would do anything to escape to my own little world and feeling that I would rather be alone, as I felt safer and untouched, with not a soul to hurt me.

To this day, when I visualise and go back to my younger self, I could feel my inner child's world was empty, and she was hurt and alone. But being alone was far better than being surrounded by people who were judgemental, people who saw other people's flaws as a win for themselves, people who failed to see and failed to appreciate the beauty in others.

This part of my childhood affected me and became this unwelcome shadow that followed me as I grew into a young woman. I wanted that feeling of hurt to go away. There were times when I was called ugly because of my skin colour. I was constantly being pointed out as different from the others, but all I could do was smile and pretend as if none of those words bothered me. The truth was it hurt me to the core. I wanted many times to just crawl in a hole and cry.

My heart was flooded with my own tears - tears that no one could see and only I could feel as I continued to swim into the journey as a helpless young child. In my mind, to cover my pain, I created this imaginary world of fairy tales friends named Cinderella, Snow White, Little Red Riding Hood, and I was always

Rapunzel. That was what I held on to, the make-believe world of peace and happiness.

Over time, I became someone with low self-esteem, someone who never feels good enough, someone who was constantly seeking validation and approval, and someone who just wanted to be accepted and be the same as everybody else and as my other siblings.

To some, I was shy, quiet and timid. The truth is I am someone who loves people and loves being surrounded by people and events. I am a person who loves to get to know everybody, a person that believes everybody has a story to tell that we can all learn and inspire from.

But, I was too young to speak, too scared to claim my position in the world that was full of adults who make it their job to poke fun at other people's expenses, belittling others because of their own small, insecure minds.

I remember sitting in front of a mirror, chanting a line quietly to myself:

> *Mirror mirror on the wall, who's the fairest one of all?*
> – Snow White

I believe I was about ten years old, and I was hungry for validation and wanting to be accepted like everybody else. So, one afternoon, I got hold of the Johnson and Johnson talcum powder. Remember the white bottle with red writing on it? I applied the powder on my entire face so that I could barely see my eyes. I applied it so thick that my whole face looked like a mountain of snow had just landed. It sounds kind of funny now, but back then, I remember the feeling of being a shattered, broken-hearted little girl as I wiped away the thick pile of white talcum powder from my eyes.

I used to fantasise that I was Rapunzel with long braided hair living up in the attic. In my own little safe imaginary world, I saw myself sitting at the edge of a window up in the attic waiting to be rescued. I thought then, as my face was white as snow, a prince would come and rescue me, whisk me away, and we live happily ever after. As silly as that sounds, that was what I used to hold on to, my own little fairy tales, my go-to place in my mind that has saved me from the hurt.

Rapunzel Saved Herself!

Fast forward to 18 years old, and I was awarded a full scholarship to study abroad. There in America in the 'Land of Opportunity', I found the 'real me'. I did my own self-discovery, and I learned to accept the person that I am and not the person I was told I was. I found the meaning of love in the absence of judgement. I refused to be imprisoned by the labels others put on me to cover up their own small thinking and ignorance.

Through my self-discovery journey, I became a woman who understands love and compassion, empathy and pain. I became a woman that could turn pain into something good and see the positives in every bad situation. I became a woman who sees beauty is simply an outer shell. I became a woman that believes in the power of forgiveness. I became a woman that was born with a much bigger purpose.

In order for me to be worthy of that purpose, I had to experience pain, as with that experience, I know how to serve what I was born to do and how I could help others better. I became a woman who believes that to be ME is ENOUGH! I revised my chant:

> *Mirror mirror on the wall, it doesn't matter if I'm short or tall,*
> *If I have skinny legs or my hips are wide, it only matters who I am inside.*
> *Blue eyes, brown eyes, black or green, what makes me beautiful can't be seen.*
> *When you look at me, don't judge me by my parts.*
> *The most beautiful thing about me is my heart!*
> *–TinyBuddha.Com*

Lost All Only To Gain More

> *Sometimes, you have to get knocked down lower than you have ever been.*
> *To stand back up taller than you ever were.*
> *– Black Veil Brides*

April 1997, alone at the Narita International Airport, Tokyo, Japan, with tears flowing down my cheeks, I began to write and put on paper with a hope to translate what was in my confused, shattered mind. I was on transit from Little Rock, Arkansas, USA, to my homeland Malaysia via Tokyo, and my flight was delayed for three hours.

I remember sitting on the floor at one of the corners, feeling alone, broken and numb, as I was trying to comprehend what had happened. The world I once knew was shattered. As I sat in my corner watching other travellers passing by going about their affairs, I saw my world in darkness.

Narita International Airport was one of the busiest airports in the world. Millions of passengers come and go. The announcements for flights departures and arrivals and paging for passengers were non-stop. Everything seemed busy and loud.

Travellers were everywhere, with some casually sitting and chatting, reading, walking from one duty-free shop to the next, and some were seen rushing to their gates with fear on their faces of the possibility of missing their flights.

I could see how hectic everything around me was, but my world was quiet and sad. I heard nothing. I was dead inside and felt like my heart was ripped apart. A big part of me was gone, taken away. My brain was paralysed, trying to make sense of everything. My mind was filled with unanswered questions. How did I get here? How could he take her away from me, knowing I was her only world and she was mine?

As I wiped away my tears, another stream of tears came rushing down my cheeks. I was unable to control my feeling of emptiness and loss. I didn't care who was watching and what they were thinking of me. All I could think was: How? Where did I go wrong? How could he took her away from me, her mother, after all these years? I was the only stability in her world. How could he be so cruel? Why should an innocent child who had nothing to do with the break-up end up being the victim of the broken relationship between couples and the system?

A thousand and one questions kept dropping into my head over and over. How was I supposed to know the decision I had made back in 1989 was going to alter my life forever? Why didn't I see this coming? I didn't deserve to be separated from her. She was just six years old. I was her world and to rob her from the only world she knew was unfair, to say the least. To shake her world and to put her through the pain of the break-up battle was beyond anyone's comprehension, let alone a child.

As I was trying to find some logic to the situation, so many thoughts flooding in, but all I could think of was: Is she okay? Is he looking after her? Is she missing me? What is she doing right now? Does she have her favourite blanket as she lays in bed at night? I sat and wondered if she knew that somewhere halfway across the world, her dear mummy was dying, missing her.

As I sobbed and as my tears fell on the paper smudging the words I had written, my mind wondered about my little princess and her innocent mind. Did she think I left without her by choice? What was she told when I was not there to tuck her in bed at night?

Not there to read her bedtime stories? Not there when she was upset, not there to kiss her and to assure that everything was going to be okay. What was she told that she was not to return to the same school she started in Jan that year? What was she told about me, her mummy? Was she ever told how much I love and adore her? Was she missing me? Did she ask for me at all, or has she forgotten me?

Then through the airport paging system, the announcements came for all passengers on Malaysia Airlines flight to Kuala Lumpur to resume boarding.

I don't remember much about my entire flight home after that, but I know not a single day without her since my trip back home was easy. Some days were unbearable. There were many nights when my tears fell down my cheeks until I fell asleep.

Emotionally and spiritually, I was bleeding pain that only I could see. My world was never the same. I was missing her beyond words. I was craving for her smell, the sound of her voice. Not having her to cuddle and hold broke me. Not seeing her smiles and hearing her cheeky giggles shattered my world.

At times, it felt like a knife that cut slowly through my heart, but I knew I had to be strong not only for me but mostly for her and the future she deserves. Knowing that she needed me was what kept me going.

Four months later, she came home to me, and for the first couple of years, it was shared custody, and in 2001, she came home for good.

Divorce and custody is never an easy process and can be highly stressful for any family. Continuous feuds and never-ending arguments in and out of court between couples add more pain.

Some adults are too focused on their own anger, hurt, and pain that they hurt their loved ones in the process. Allowing emotions and focusing on the problems after any break-ups only prolong the pain and slow down the healing process.

I have learned to allow time to ease our disagreements, and time did eventually sort us out for the better for my daughter and me. When we learn to let pain, hurt and anger heal, we open up to more goodness in our lives. By doing so, we gain more and the ability to smell the beauty of life again.

Do What's Best For Me – Celebrate My Many 'FIRSTs'

To be what I am today and for me to accept me and all of me, has certainly not an overnight process. It was a process of many discoveries, many moments of self-reflecting, acknowledging the pain I endured and facing the many years of hurt and feeling of being told I was not good enough.

I made a conscious choice that I could either rise above it or give others the power to dictate my future. I know wholeheartedly, I have everything to be thankful for, nothing about me to be sorry for. Through my own journey of self-help, I knew I have the ability to define my own reality. I have learnt to accept that we are not in control of others' thoughts, but we are in control of our thoughts.

I learnt to become aware of who I am. I learnt to always remind myself of all the achievements I have had, big or small, and to reward myself even with the small achievements as they are significant in my eyes - from receiving a full paid scholarship, to learning how to speak English, to going to America.

I have also learned to appreciate and be blessed with my many 'firsts'. The first Asian born at my University to be crowned Miss Homecoming Queen; the first within my family to have and graduate with a degree from a university outside of my home country; and the first in my family to have the guts and get divorced and to accept that being divorced isn't a tragedy.

Okay, some may not regard divorce as an achievement to celebrate the 'first' for; but it was to me as it symbolised the strength I possess and the many lessons I have learned, especially about the importance of being financially independent.

> *Today expect something good to happen to you no matter what occurred yesterday.*
> *Realise the past no longer holds you captive.*
> *It can only continue to hurt you if you hold on to it.*
> *Let the past go. A simply abundant world awaits.*
> *– Sarah Ban Breathnach*

'You Have a Gift BUT It's Not Yours to Keep'

Everything in life has a lesson if we choose to see it. You can choose to play the victim and blame everybody else for everything negative that happened to you, or you can choose to learn from the experience and choose how to respond to what has happened to you and rise above it.

I have had my fair share of negatives and challenges. I could spend hours and days listing them if I want to. But what benefit is that going to serve me or anyone around me?

So I learned to magnify and be grateful for all the positives I have been blessed with. I am grateful for everyone I have met to date, especially those who have brought out the best in me. These many amazing people are the ones I will never forget. They were the ones who listened without judgement, loved me without conditions, and they were the ones who reminded me why I am worth it.

I am still a work in progress. Some days I still am a little affected and do doubt myself. But I know when that triggers, I catch myself and whisper to my inner self, '5 4 3 2 1….breath Suze, do not allow those who don't matter to rip your power away.'

I recall someone I used to know, who I looked up to, saying, 'Simba *(the name he gave me)*, you have a special gift, but that gift is not yours to keep. It is for you to share with others, so they are not deprived.'

His words that day are what has kept me rising to become who I am today. He is one of the many beautiful souls who accepted me, listened without judgement and taught me how to love without conditions.

I believe that if I was to dwell on and allow the hurt that others have caused me to continue to hurt me, then I would be allowing myself to be a victim. This would be selfish, only thinking of myself as, 'Oh poor me...'

The truth is I know I have so much more to be grateful for. So I don't give myself permission to feel less of what I am. I have learned to be unapologetically ME! I believe that I can create my own reality. I forgive those who have hurt me but not for them; the forgiveness is for me.

I have a bigger purpose in life. People experience hurt each and every day. The beauty of that is, as humans, we have choices. We can choose to live with hurt, to continuously carry the pain, or we can choose to find the courage as we all have the ability to heal and forgive!

Jr Ridinger, a founder of Shop.com, whom I look up to, famously said, '*You must succeed so other people can realise their dream*'. Now I live by that quote in everything that I do. I now take my past experiences, past hurts and past judgements that were made upon me, as wisdom, strength, and lessons learned.

No Room for Hate and Negativity

As humans, we tend to make the negatives bigger than they actually are. We feel that by talking more about them, it justifies the pain. Laying blame is so easy, but doing so feeds more negativity, and over time I feel that it gives us the excuses to play small and to play the victim.

The truth is we are only hurting ourselves, giving the power to the negatives that serve no purpose and some of those negatives are beyond our control. By indulging and entertaining some things that don't make sense, we are robbing us of our time, robbing us of our ability to see the good in ourselves and how that good could shine in others in the process. It's time we shift our focus more on the good and let the good shine in our lives!

When life gives you lemons
Say thank you
Make lemonade
Plant a lemon tree
Use it to spice up your meals
Learn to juggle
Sell them.
-Initially coined by Elbert Hubbard

Love ME Tender Love ME Sweet

So today, I am proud to say that I am comfortable being wrapped in my own skin; happily being me and being me is ENOUGH.

Yes, I AM ENOUGH.

I am blessed with what I have around me. I am blessed with those who love me for everything that I am. Every day I get to wake up to greet the world is another day of opportunity to live, love, learn and contribute.

My aim is to live in the moment, love beyond words, and laugh as much as I breathe!

To this day, I make my bed every morning immediately after waking up. Yup, ironically, that is how I begin my day. It's that simple. What started as a chore that my Ma made me do when I was young, is now my morning ritual.

Making my bed every morning gives me a sense of pride. As insane as it sounds, to see my bed nicely made gives me a great feeling of achievement to go on completing the other tasks that I set for the rest of my day. With a nice hot cuppa sprinkled with what I called my 'chocolate fairy dust', and together with my go-to 'lipstick', is how I begin my day and has been my number one key to my sanity and success.

My journey now is to share my life experiences, the lessons I have learned to empower and inspire others. I am fulfilled with everything I am and everything that I have. My journey forward is to help others around me, especially other women.

With the skills I am blessed with, it is my passion to offer support and guidance so they, too, can live a contented and happy life. I thanked my mama for the many words of wisdom she gave me.

Money and Lipstick summarise my mantra. We all need a place we feel safe. A place we like to think is ours. I don't know what it is, but lipstick somehow always magically gives me the safe place, the joy as my mama said it would. With that joy, I have learned to look at every challenge, big or small, from a much healthier lense.

On a good day, as soon as I have a lipstick on, my confidence level rises. I feel taller, I am calmer to face my day, and whatever comes my way. On a day that is not so kind, lipstick helps me to be grateful for the good that is already present in my life. It helps me to also acknowledge any goals I have achieved and the changes I have seen in myself. And ohhhhh, having a made-up bed to go home to, especially on the days that are not so kind, feels so good!

What you think, you become.
What you feel, you attract.
What you imagine, you create.
-Buddha

Money & Lipstick 'Be Gutsy, Make a Difference and Pave the Way for Others'

My mama never had the opportunity to create her own financial independence, the way she wanted to. I know there was so much she wanted to achieve but did not have the resources to do so. The era she grew up in, the culture she was raised in, was challenging. Having an open mind was frowned upon as women. Despite the world she lived in at the time, Mama was successful in her own right. Though she was not fortunate enough to attend higher education, somehow, against the odds, she managed to start a couple of successful businesses from the few dollars she saved from what was left from the family's daily household budget.

In my eyes, she was a gutsy woman. Not only was she gutsy, but she also made a difference in her own community. Through her many challenges and obstacles, she used her strength and that paved the way for others.

She made the obstacles her reasons to pursue and overcome them. She empowered other women in her community to use the obstacles as a ladder to succeed. She inspired those who thought dreams belong only in their sleep, to keep believing in their dreams, and to go after them.

Mama has a gutsy heart and a gutsy mind. Despite her many struggles and pain, she showered everyone around her with tremendous love and beauty. She carried with her a beautiful glow and light that allowed others to shine as well. She was born with a gift to make everyone around her to feel happy.

Her contagious laugh could brighten up any room. Mama treated everyone the same. Being around her made you feel special. She gathered her strength from distress. She turned something that was not possible, and she made it possible. Through her ability to heal and forgive, Mama discovered beauty. Mama never lost her self-worth. She saw love in places others didn't see existed. Her determination and belief in herself were based on her own mind, and she was not at all affected by the outside events. That, to me, was GUTSY!

I choose:

> To *live by choice, not by chance.*
> To *be motivated, not manipulated.*
> To *be useful, not used.*
> To *make changes, not excuses.*
> To *excel, not compete.*
> *I choose self-esteem, not self-pity.*
> *I choose my inner voice, not the random opinions of others.*
> -Miranda Marrott

Be Unapologetically YOU!

Being gutsy, to me, is about not playing small. Being gutsy is about stepping into who we are meant to be.

Being gutsy is about believing that we are meant for greater things. Being gutsy is about accepting that defeat is a choice, and it is a choice to not accept defeat.

Being gutsy is about giving ourselves permission to make mistakes. Being gutsy is about acceptance – acceptance of you and others.

Being gutsy is about being okay to love yourself first. Being gutsy is about embracing the moment we have today, letting go of the past, forgiving those who have hurt you.

Being gutsy is about learning from the experience and not allowing the past to define you.

Being gutsy is wanting to be better and taking steps to do better. Being gutsy is about sharing your knowledge with others around you and giving with no expectations in return.

Being gutsy is not making it about you. Being gutsy is about others.

Being gutsy is about making a difference. Being gutsy is about paving the way for others while we remain humble and grateful. Being gutsy is about believing in the power of love, the power of compassion.

Being gutsy is to be unapologetically YOU!

What We Discovered

In this final chapter, the co-authors share the three key insights they discovered along their journey.

This acts not only as a summary of what they have written about in their chapters, but as practical advice you can use to assist you in your own personal discovery and development journey.

The authors in this book are not experts. They are all regular people, overcoming their own difficulties and hurdles, to pursue their dreams and goals, and live more truly being who they are.

Every co-author's journey to discover more of themselves, to be more themselves, has been different, and that is perhaps how it should be.

Every journey is a personal one, and these short summaries may help you understand their journeys. You may even see yourself reflected in some of them.

We hope that in sharing these insights, you will be inspired to resolve any limiting beliefs you may have, follow your own dreams and passions, discover who you really are and be you.

Antoinette Pellegrini

- ❖ **Unbecome what you are not.** Sometimes the process of becoming you involves shedding who you are not. We often take on other people's expectations, and certainly when we are young, other people's values and beliefs. We are also affected by our own limiting beliefs that we developed when very young – beliefs around our interpretation of what happened to us. These beliefs are often negative; that we aren't good enough, that we are not lovable or worthy. Being yourself involves shedding all of the these limiting beliefs to reveal who you really are.

- ❖ **Change only happens when you do something differently.** If you keep repeating patterns, especially relationship patterns, then you only get more of the same. Change is often difficult and it's easy to stay in your comfort zone, but often our comfort zones are not very comfortable. Recognise the patterns that don't serve you and decide to make changes, approach things differently, and other opportunities and possibilities will open for you.

- ❖ **Transformation is never easy but always worthwhile.** It takes courage and perseverance to take the risk to change, transform and grow. The process can be difficult, but the reward is immense. You become who you were always meant to be.

Francis Borg

- ❖ **Never stop learning.** I always loved learning and never so much more when I realised that I am a very interesting subject to me. Whatever course I have taken, even relationship and couples courses, I have found that I have always learnt more about myself.

- ❖ **Our lives can be so much more when we know ourselves better.** The courses and all the roads I took led me to discover that I needed more information about myself, about why I became a person with beliefs of not belonging, of being alone and lonely. This continued until I allowed a safer connection and experienced the positive benefits from the couples workshop I attended.

- ❖ **Your relationship is a two way GIFT and you really MATTER.** I am happily connected with my husband and all our children, and when a difference or disconnection shows up, we now have the skills to discuss and repair our connections. While my husband and I model how we get on, we are modelling to our children and grandchildren how to be safe, stay connected and repair when upsets and ruptures happen. And ruptures and upsets do sometimes still happen; they are just much further apart. Our skills have become second nature, and we are better listeners and ask for more information.

Sothi de Boer

❖ **Life forms, life's form**. When I was 12 years old, my Year 6 geography textbook had the most beautiful photograph of the Murray Darling Basin. I will always treasure the memory of my mother's reminder that I had once told her that I will live there one day. My life changed in the form of a jet plane and one suitcase.

Always envision what you love. You never know when it may come true.

❖ **The alchemy of movement.** The sound of aeroplanes overhead always had me looking skywards, my imagination soaring wild of the rich and wealthy, holding the big bird still and clouds drifting by. But the aeroplane always flew away and the clouds stood still.

From the day I placed a map of Melbourne down on the pavement of the corner of Bourke and Swanston Streets and a kind old gentleman knelt down beside me and helped me orientate myself, I knew I had found my place. This corner is where I began my first employment as a Merchandising Assistant in the Ladies Buying Department of Coles.

Look to see where you find your stillness, movement and your place in the world.

- ❖ **Self defining moments.** University changed me. The four years were certainly not easy but I did it. It taught me resilience. Life does not have to be easy. To choose to remain in Australia was not easy. I chose change and independence. My family in Malaysia will always be very dear to me. My husband and children are my wildest safest place. I am home. Look to see what defines you and embrace what you call home.

Suze Elford

- **We may not control all the events that happen to us.** We can either let them define our worth and allow them to determine what they think is best for us or we can decide not to be reduced by them and be the hero of our own story.

- **While money doesn't guarantee us happiness, without money, we are limited in choices.** So, stay savvy and stay in control of your finances so you can be more prepared for the unexpected.

- **We are all born with tremendous potential to do great and meaningful things.** As we discover our true purpose in life, facing moments of successes and failures, moments of adversity, our characters are built. So find your why, find what inspires you, what motivates you and what gives you great fulfilment. Strive to be better than you were yesterday. Stop playing small; instead, step into who you are meant to be. Embrace adversity as a chance for opportunity and growth. Be the best you, be gutsy, make a difference, and pave the way for others.

Johanna Elizabeth

- **Keep on keeping on.** Just put one foot in front of the other, and keep going. You can do this. It was keeping busy that helped me cope, as well as the distractions and sometimes the help of a supportive person, whether a friend or counsellor. I believe that my inner power and the desire to improve myself pushed me to keep going, as did my positive self-talk, 'I can do this', and 'Everything will be alright'.

- **Nothing lasts forever, so take opportunities when they come your way.** Sometimes a tiny window of opportunity appears; take it if it leads you to where you want to go. You never know where the opportunity may take you, and it is always a chance to learn and grow.

- **Prioritise your own health.** Take that day off if you feel unwell, physically or mentally because burnout is real. Once you have burned out, it's extra hard to get your mojo back. On looking back over my childhood, marriage, study, relationships and work, I realised I had been pushing myself and spreading myself too thin. Consider your own needs and your own health.

Lesley Lennon

- **It is human nature to want to have control over every aspect of our lives.** The reality is we cannot. How we react when this truth is presented to us can be surprising. We learn so much about ourselves when we are challenged and made to feel uncomfortable.

- **We can, to some extent, choose how we view challenging situations.** It is the ability to chose whether to focus on the negative and the positive aspects of a situation that allows us to grow, learn and change.

- **Nothing stays the same forever.** Gratitude is an important aspect of being a healthy individual. Challenging times encourage us to identify where our gratitude comes from. They remind us that we need to be more reflective and grateful for the blessings we have. With the busyness of life, we often forget this pivotal point.

Lynne Owens

- **Never underestimate the power of the mind through illness.** Set your intention; you don't need to be the victim; you can be YOU.

  I wouldn't go as far as to say that my cancer journey has been a gift, but it has given me some valuable lessons and reminded me how powerful the mind can be. I don't think we are really aware of our limits until we are forced to explore them and find out how resilient and adaptable we can be when we need to.

- **Say YES to those who offer to support you along the way, even if it's uncomfortable – it's not a weakness, it courageous.** I don't know if my friends and others who supported me know how grateful and appreciative I was for their kindness and generosity – it helped me on a myriad of levels, and I loved every minute of it. I also have deep gratitude for the support from my amazing friends.

- **Trust your intuition. Be BRAVE, challenge the system, do what is best for you.** During the two years of my cancer journey, I met with a host of individuals, including specialists, doctors, nurses, surgeons, oncologists, hospital staff, wig consultants and exercise physiologists, with some relationships a lot more challenging than others.

I recognised how strong and resilient I was. I questioned, challenged and engaged in robust discussion when I felt it was warranted, although not necessarily welcomed. I was not your typical cancer patient. I was unrelenting in my expectations and assertive and demanding with hospital staff in order to make the process work for me.

Sal Prothero

- **New experiences come with new growth - your way of thinking expands and you discover more about yourself.** For me, living in different countries took me out of my comfort zone and into new surroundings and experiences that reset my body and mind. The challenge of being the 'newbie', of experiencing new things, increases your curiosity and expands your personal growth.

- **Anything can be achieved if you set your mind to it.** Most of us have fear and if we let it rule our lives, we won't achieve our goals. Have the courage to take on new experiences and follow your passion and what you want from life.

- **Make your health a priority.** You can't live your life to the full if you have poor health. There are so many factors involved in ill health, depression, anxiety, and mental health issues, such as environment, lifestyle, mindset, past and present stressors, biological processes but diet and nutrition still play a big part.

My philosophy is to start with the diet and lifestyle – small changes make a big difference.

Diane Psaila

- **Embrace the spirit of empowerment.** I feel it is important to focus on the will to start each day with a clean slate by injecting positive thinking to empower thought processes that will set the tone for what comes next.

  I think of the warm and all-encompassing inspirational influences that I am drawn to in life. Precious individuals who nurture a mindset of excitement and challenge giving me hope and encouragement to push out at my comfort zone and explore what's possible.

- **Face challenges and remember to maintain your self-respect and live authentically.** Of course, there's going to be the conflicting flip-side too, of unsettling situations that present themselves, hovering in mind space, at times overwhelming and threatening, testing the depths of emotional and logical spheres.

  I believe overcoming this involves a conscious mindset of rising to the challenge, of conceding acceptance in differences of opinion or alternatively, standing firm, steadfast in moral beliefs; each emerging at a fulfilling place of clarity, strength, wisdom, and above all, a demonstration of respect of self and others. This is the ultimate show of goodwill and authenticity.

- ❖ **Fear is unsettling, but it can help define perspectives and revelations.** When the COVID-19 pandemic launched its lethal attack on the world in 2020, all that was once familiar became unstuck in an instant and in its place emerged a foreign all-engrossing fear; of mounting sickness, death and loss of livelihoods.

  Interestingly though, for me, blessed with the luxury of confinement in my beautiful nature inspired home, it also offered a haven for reflection and a means to harness a natural strength to adapt to change and hold onto a sense of direction and well-being.

  It was a welcome diversion to the hustle and bustle of keeping up appearances and the sense of urgency of needing to be somewhere else. Time slowed; the little things that quite often were fleetingly acknowledged or were overlooked all together with preoccupation, became the big things and there was an immense grounding appreciation and comfort in that awareness.

Dawn Sulley

- ❖ **Respect your heritage but don't let it define you.** I believe your roots set your path in your formative years. Anyone who lets this restrict their aspirations in adulthood does themselves a great disservice. In my case, this involved moving into a career in the Aged Care Industry.

- ❖ **Follow your passions, stay positive no matter what**. Throughout your life journey, people will question your intentions and your goals, often in very negative terms. It is your journey, so follow your passions.

  A positive frame of mind is the biggest single asset you can bring to your endeavours no matter what aspect of your life you are dealing with - the good, the bad and the indifferent.

- ❖ **Stay true to your dreams.** Let your dreams be your inspiration and your guiding light. Fulfilling your dreams is always a work in progress, it will be your life's greatest achievement..

Heather Thorne

- ❖ **There are things you can only know about living in a new place when you get there.** That's part of the adventure. Some things may be harder than you had anticipated; others will be beyond anything you could imagine. My adventure in moving to Melbourne has made me grow as a woman.

- ❖ **Make the move now – there will never be the perfect time anyway.** Once you've made the decision to move, commit to it and pack your bags. Looking back over the last three years since moving to Melbourne, life has certainly been an adventure! It hasn't all been smooth sailing but, even at my lowest point, I didn't consider returning to Perth. Melbourne is my home now. If you want to move, have courage and do it.

- ❖ **Moving can be scary but staying still is scarier.** Make the move so you don't have regrets that you were too scared to follow your dreams. Having the courage to move cities at 57 and follow my dream has given me a strong belief in myself. I am now confident that I can achieve any goal I set myself.

Caterina Zanca

- **Be determined and never give up.** I gave up so many times until I broke the habit of giving in and giving up. We need to break old habits and put in place new ones so our brains can learn a new way of healthy thinking.

  I found myself ready and in the right headspace and embraced the new changes in me, such as my strengths and improving my lifestyle. I feel reborn again

- **Be Focused. Always keep your eyes on the prize.** It is what I did to become healthier and drop five dress sizes. Sometimes we need a push or a wake-up call to change some aspects of our lives.

  This can, and often does come, from a positive or negative comment someone makes. However, what I have realised is that all along, it was up to me to take charge of my life and not rely on what people thought about me. I should have respected myself, I feel, no matter what size I was or how I lived my life.

- **Be triumphant and enjoy your success.** I found my self-respect, confidence and have maintained my weight loss for over a year – something I have never achieved before.

  When you feel great and confident about yourself, you radiate that to people around you, and nothing but positiveness can come out of that. There will always be shallow people out there who judge us, but you are the only truthful judge of yourself.

Author Bios

Antoinette Pellegrini, Johanna Elizabeth, Suze Elford, Lynne Owens
Caterina Zanca, Sal Prothero, Sothi de Boer, Diane Psaila
Heather Thorne, Lesley Lennon, Francis Borg, Dawn Sulley

Antoinette Pellegrini

Antoinette Pellegrini lives in a leafy Melbourne suburb in Victoria, Australia.

She is an Author, Teacher, Writing Coach and Holistic Therapist.

She raised two amazing young men as a single mother and overcame many hardships and challenges throughout her life.

Rejecting established religions, Antoinette discovered her own version of spirituality, a mix of quantum physics and metaphysics, a combination of science and spirituality, that she used to make sense of the world.

For many years, Antoinette dreamt of becoming an author, writing self-help, motivational and inspirational books, on awareness of self, who you really are, your connection to others and everything around you. Her message is that the key to creating the life you love rests with your thoughts - your thoughts matter - and being conscious of how your thinking affects your life, allows you to be a conscious creator in control of how you respond to the circumstances of your life.

In 2017, her dream came true with the publication of her first book, *Your Thoughts Matter: The Future You Are Creating Starts Now,* and the accompanying *Reflection*

Journal and Affirmation Cards. They contain 25 Reflections and Affirmations on connection and the power of positive thinking and conscious choice. It is designed to empower and inspire the reader to create the life they would like to live.

Antoinette followed this with the creation of an award-winning anthology series called *We Inspire Now*. Antoinette created this anthology series in the hope of inspiring people to look within themselves, heal past hurts, and have the courage to pursue and achieve their goals.

Book One in the anthology series, *Live Your Truth,* featured regular people who were daring to follow their dreams and help inspire others to do the same.

In Book Two, *A Message to Your Younger Self: What Would You Say?,* authors shared the messages they would have wanted to receive when they were young, thereby enabling them to heal past hurts and shed limiting beliefs.

Both Book One and Book Two have been award-winning finalists in the 2019 and 2021 International Book Awards run by the American Book Fest.

This anthology, *Journey To Me,* is the third book in Antoinette's *We Inspire Now*. It explores what it means to be yourself, live more fully being you, and uncover who you really are.

Antoinette next project is to publish her children's book *Sandcastles: A Story About Our Connected World* later in 2021. It depicts some of the concepts in her book *Your Thoughts Matter*, particularly our connection with everyone and everything in our world. It also touches on the subject of death and eternal renewal and growth.

Antoinette is also a secondary school teacher, working as a teacher for several years before starting a corporate career. Antoinette left the corporate world in 2016 to follow her passion for writing and helping others find their voice and achieve their personal goals.

Antoinette has helped people achieve their personal goals, improve their wellbeing, energy levels and happiness. As a writing and publishing coach, she has enabled people to make their dreams of being published authors a reality. Her focus is on the link between mind, body and spirit and the critical part the mind plays in relation to overall health, wellbeing and achievement of goals.

Antoinette offers one on one consultations, motivational coaching, personal development and writing workshops and courses.

www.antoinettepellegrini.com
www.weinspirenowbooks.com
Email: antoinettepellegriniauthor@gmail.com

www.facebook.com/authorantoinettepellegrini
Phone: +61 438056085

Francis Borg

Francis Borg was born in and grew up in Blacktown NSW. After finishing school, she undertook a nursing cadetship at Blacktown Hospital and became a registered general nurse.

During a working holiday in Darwin, she met her future husband, Ian. After Francis completed midwifery studies, they were married in 1981.

Darwin was their first home, then four months after their marriage, Ian's employer asked them to move to Indonesia, which began a five year period of living overseas. Following two years in Java, Indonesia, Francis lived in Samoa, Kiribati and Fiji. Francis and Ian had two children in Indonesia, and their third child was born in Fiji.

Upon returning to Australia in late 1986, they first lived in Gladstone Qld, then until 1994 also lived in Clare Weir (North Qld), Sunshine Coast, back to Darwin, then back to Sunshine Coast.

A fourth child was born in Gladstone, and a fifth in Darwin. Brisbane became home in 1994 and remains home today. From 1994 to 2015, Francis worked for several employers, based around her being a registered nurse and midwife, including Queensland Health, Wesley Mission and Uniting Care.

Between 1995 and 2006, Francis pursued further studies, through which she attained a graduate diploma in Theology and a masters degree in Social Science (Pastoral Counselling). Over that time, she was has trained and volunteered with SIDs and Kids, and Catholic Psychiatric Pastoral Care and Communidade Edmund Rice, East Timor.

The couple's sixth child was born in 2003. In 2006 Francis established her own small business as a counsellor and family therapist, which grew into Brisbane North Counselling.

After being introduced to Imago relationship therapy in 2012, she undertook ongoing training and development in Imago in Australia, USA, New Zealand and South Africa, so that today she is an internationally certified Imago relationship therapist and couples workshop presenter. Francis is also registered in Australia and accredited as a Clinical Member by PACFA.

Brisbane North Counselling
127 Roscommon Road,
Boondall.4034
0406 949 921

www.brisbanenorthcounselling.com.au
www.brisbaneimagorelationshipcounselling.com/test-page-workshops
francis@brisbanenorthcounselling.com.au

Sothi de Boer

Sothi de Boer is Malaysian of Sri Lankan descent. Her father migrated from Sri Lanka as a young boy, and her mother is Malaysian born.

Sothi's education in Kuantan, a coastal town on the east coast of mainland Malaysia, at the Assunta Convent Primary School and a Methodist Girls Secondary School, was in the English medium.

Sothi came to Melbourne in February 1974 to continue her studies. Her transition to tertiary studies in Australia was blessed, smooth and easy. Sothi is forever indebted to Gough Whitlam for this privilege and opportunity.

A Bachelor of Science Degree transformed her destiny and empowered her to work in Australia, adopt a new homeland and become its citizen.

Sothi finished her working career as a Medical Scientist and now enjoys immersing herself in an education of all that evaded her during her busy years.

Suze Elford

Born in Malaysia, Suze was taught that education is key, and to be financially independent is important for women.

Her late mom was her role model who instilled in her that when life throws us a curveball, we choose how we react to it. She taught Suze to expect the best but be prepared for the worst.

Upon finishing high school, Suze was awarded a full scholarship to further her education. Her first passport was literally her passport to her future as she travelled for the first time on her own, thousands of miles away from her homeland to the USA to study.

After graduating from the University of Arkansas, Suze worked for a Fortune 500 company in Missouri, USA, to pursue her career as a Business and Financial Analyst.

Suze is happily married to Andrew, her Aussie country boy from Victoria and from 1998, Suze calls Australia home.

Suze left her corporate career to be a full time mum to her two children Sasha and Ben. When her youngest

Ben started high school, Suze began her entrepreneurial journey.

With zero business experience and only her determination and clear purpose and intention, Suze founded her first business, an event management company called Table Talk Sydney.

She has since owned a couple of other successful businesses under her corporate umbrella of Sincerely Suze.

In Jan 2020, after becoming an empty nester, Suze and her husband Andrew decided to change their lifestyle from the hustle and bustle of '4 Seasons in One Day' Melbourne, to a more laid back, 'Beautiful One Day, Perfect The Next' Queensland.

Combining her passion with numbers, her corporate and business experiences and her life journey, Suze is now a Money and Personal Development Coach. She helps women to have a healthier relationship with money and helps them to find their true purpose in life.

On a non-serious side, Suze would travel anywhere for a great Asian food, her heritage. She's a big advocate in making her bed first thing in the morning as the best way to start the day.

Music is her therapy. Her happy place is cruising in her car. She dances to be lost in the moment and to nurture her love for life.

Suze is great at managing different roles, from a mum, a wife, a partner, a sister, a friend, a business mentor, a boss lady, you name it; she is very productive that way. Suze also loves to learn from others' journey, and her mantra is to be better than she was yesterday.

To learn more about Suze, please go to:
www.moneyandlipstick.com
Instagram: moneyandlipstick
Instagram: sincerelysuze
LinkedIn: Suze Elford

To shop and get paid:
www.sincerelysuze.com.au
www.sincerelysuze.com

Johanna Elizabeth

Johanna Elizabeth was born in Holland following the war, the youngest of five children.

They say it takes three generations to become free of the horrors of war. So as a second-generation member of a war-damaged family, Johanna is now watching proudly her three children live in a free democracy.

Having become a single parent while her children were very young, she is a very proud and passionate mum and grandmother. Her children are now all well established and married with beautiful, healthy children of their own.

Growing up as a migrant child had its challenges. Having started her life in Australia in a migrant camp was difficult. Her mother was frequently ill, so Johanna often had to manage on her own.

Through numerous jobs and experiences, Johanna finally became a registered nurse. She studied hard and achieved extra certificates. This assisted her in trying to be the best nurse she could be. It was not without trials and tribulations.

Having written notes as a way of coping throughout her years, it was easy to put this story of struggles and achievements together. Johanna's inner strength made her strong and determined to achieve what was planned.

Hopefully, this story will assist others to tap into that inner power we all have.

Contact:

Joelizabeth51@gmail.com

Lesley Lennon

Lesley Lennon is the proud mother of Kara, Grace and Ben. She is also a doting grandmother to her grandson Vinnie.

As a young child Lesley had a nomadic lifestyle. She and her mother, father and two sisters moved regularly from home to home in Metropolitan Melbourne, country Victoria and on occasion, interstate with her father's jobs as a Retail Store Manager.

When Lesley was 12 years old her family settled permanently in a suburb North of Melbourne's CBD. There she completed her High School years, met her husband Stephen whom she later married and bought their first home.

Prior to having children Lesley began her fulltime working life at the State Bank of Victoria. When she became a mother, she initially chose to stay at home to care for them and later as they grew older worked in the field of Hospitality. At the age of 39 Lesley went back to University to obtain her Bachelor of Education at RMIT University with Distinction.

Lesley spent many years passionately teaching Primary school children. She gained great satisfaction from seeing her students develop, grow and learn to their full potential.

She has a keen interest in Spirituality Personal Development, Writing, Travel, Health and Wellbeing. Lesley will always endeavour to continue to explore and learn more about herself and her areas of interest.

Lynne Owens

Lynne grew up in the North-East suburbs of Melbourne. As a young adult, she moved to St Kilda and several inner-city suburbs before settling in the leafy suburb of Montmorency.

Lynne started her working life as a professional dancer and had the opportunity to work in Japan and Australia. The friendships she established during her time in Japan are as strong as they were over 35 years ago.

During her time in Japan, Lynne discovered her love and passion for travel and language. She went back to school as a mature aged student and completed BA in languages, with a major in Japanese and Italian studies. This study was undertaken over seven years part-time whilst working full-time.

Following her dancing career, Lynne has enjoyed a variety of roles in a diverse range of industries, including Arts and Entertainment, Sports Management, Financial Conferencing, Government and Health and was fortunate to travel to the US for work. After many years in the corporate world, Lynne had a yearning for further study and embarked on a journey to become a Reflexologist.

She still works in the corporate world, commuting to Brisbane most weeks, but still finds time to see Reflexology clients in Melbourne and has recently become a Board Director for the Reflexology Association of Australia. Reflexology has also helped Lynne discover her spiritual side and passion for healing, and she is incredibly grateful for the wonderful teachers and peers she has encountered and assisted with her growth over the years. Lynne is interested in self-development and plans to undertake further studies.

Lynne is most happy when travelling and experiencing new cultures. She has a love for Japan and Spain and has returned to both countries several times and has completed the Camino de Santiago, taking five weeks and over 1,000kms to complete the walk across Spain. Other highlights were hiking in the Andes to the amazing lost city of Machu Picchu and visiting the Amazon in Peru for her 40th birthday, a driving holiday around Morocco, visiting the magical kingdom of Bhutan, and celebrating her 50th birthday with her sisters in Laos.

Lynne has always thought she would write but was not sure what the right topic would be. After receiving a diagnosis of a life-threatening illness, Lynne decided to write about her experience navigating that journey as a single person and hopes she can inspire others in the same situation to put themselves first, be strong enough to challenge the system, and go with a plan that suits their lifestyle. Lynne is now considering expanding her short story into a book.

Sal Prothero

Sal Prothero is an author, presenter and certified Clinical Nutritionist.

Originally from Ireland, Sal immigrated to Melbourne 11 years ago and now lives in the beautiful Bayside area with her husband and two teenagers. She left Ireland at the age of 19 and lived in London and Scotland before moving to Australia. Her travels motivated her to write this chapter about always being the 'newbie' in a foreign country and overcoming the challenges involved. Her determination and perseverance have enabled her to live the life that she wants to lead.

Sal and her family moved to Australia for a better lifestyle and working environment. In the UK, Sal suffered from SAD (Seasonal Affective Disorder), and her husband often worked away. Sal doesn't see her family in Ireland and the UK as much as she would like but is fortunate that her mother visits each year.

Sal worked in the corporate world in London in extremely busy and stressful roles. She always felt 'under the weather' and suffered from anxiety and depression at times. In her 30s and after her first child, she finally decided to seek help. Through her own journey, she discovered 'food as medicine' and made the decision to study a degree in Nutritional Medicine so that she could help others.

She is the founder of Whole Food Nutrition, a company that specialises in gut and mental health where she helps adolescents and adults beat depression, anxiety and ADHD with her diet, lifestyle and mindset techniques. She has also authored a chapter in *Changemakers* about how she overcame depression and anxiety.

Sal is passionate about educating people on the power of whole food and how to take control of their health. She has created her own *Feed Your Body and Mind and Happy Gut, Happy Brain* workshops and seminars, which she has presented to audiences in Melbourne.

Sal offers one on one consultations, online programs and speaking engagements.

Website: www.wholefoodnutrition.com.au
Email: sal@wholefoodnutrition.com.au

Diane Psaila

Diane Psaila lives in the north-east leafy fringe of Melbourne and has primarily followed a rewarding career in customer relations and office administration.

A mother of adult children; two sons, a daughter, and delighted to have recently become a grandmother, Diane's proud devotion to the well-being of her precious family has been a gratifying occupation.

Since her adolescent years, Diane has enjoyed reading and writing, envisioning that one day her ambition to become a published author would come to fruition.

Juggling a balance of nurturing care of her young children and earning a living, Diane also worked successfully at completing a writing course, claiming, 'It has given me a new lease on life; a welcome perspective and a will to never give up on making dreams a reality.' With this mantra, Diane has consistently taken on business study courses to improve on her skillset demonstrating that discipline teamed with aptitude will result in a successful result.

Diane's life has shown that it is full of twists and turns; the challenges at times hard to overcome and the opportunities test her courage to then set the scene for what comes next. Diane recalls fondly her role as Alumni President of her old secondary school that eventuated from sending through her peer year reunion reflection and photographs to the newly appointed Principal.

An invitation to afternoon tea set the wheels in motion for Diane who enjoyed the years that followed showcasing her creative abilities, engaging with past students, interviewing, designing and writing content for publications. A satisfying endorsement to contribute to the power of inclusive connection.

It was while Diane was interviewing an old school friend to include in a publication that her life took on another exciting turn. A published author and about to embark on creating an anthology self-help series, her friend revealed that she was seeking suitable candidates to contribute a chapter in her book titled, *Live Your Truth*. Later that year, Diane recalls the exhilaration of holding the book and opening to her chapter titled, *Imagine Spring Blossoms; A Renewed Awakening*, 'It feels surreal, and utterly rewarding.'

Diane's contribution and collaboration as a co-author continued in the second anthology, *A Message to Your Younger Self: What Would You Say?* Her chapter titled, *Jump in Puddles: Releasing My Inner Child* became the perfect antidote to set her chapter up in the third anthology, *Journey to Me*. It has signified the vital development in aligning belief systems with proactive authenticity. Diane's chapter titled, *Wings of Wonder; Lessons of Journey*, paints a picture in the reader's mind.

It delves into the pros and cons of influences that conflict interpretations and the ensuing importance of maintaining a positive attitude.

In her chapters, Diane's messages aim to nourish the soul, like enveloping a good deed, misgiving or hurt with a newfound energy to enhance, protect and urge a fulfilling way forward adding a greater dimension to the thinking process and reinforcing that self-worth is heightened by living authentically.

The power of the subconscious mind is one to embrace; its internal dialogue and depths of the journey is a masterpiece of ingenuity at play. With steely intensity, it is capable of colliding with the conscious world like a jolt of enlightenment offering its manifest of aura and insights.
Diane Psaila, 22 January 2021

Dawn Sulley

Dawn and her second husband have eight adult children and twelve grandchildren between them and have set up a home in Beautiful East Gippsland.

Dawn has worked in the aged care industry as a Diversional Therapist. For most of her adult life, she found herself seeking to teach others wanting to join the industry. Although she was grateful to the industry for giving her the stability and security she needed as a Lifestyle coordinator and the skills to move up through the ranks, she knew it didn't align with who she was.

Dawn decided to complete a teaching qualification and became a vocational teacher, and started teaching students in Ageing & Support and Leisure & Health. With this new qualification, she set out to explore her options, and along with her husband, moved to Melbourne, where she started working for the TAFE sector. Vocational teaching requires working in the industry, so she applied for a lifestyle coordination position at Alfred Health.

She was in her element and loved working in both jobs. After a few months, Dawn became unwell, finding it hard to get out of bed each morning. There was a constant pain in her right side, so her doctor sent her for an abdominal scan. Everything changed that day. She was told she had high-grade serious Ovarian Cancer. Through genome testing and research, it was found Dawn had the BRACA gene 2 mutation in one of her tumours. This allowed her to start on a maintenance program post-chemo which has been keeping her cancer at bay. Dawn has remained positive throughout this rollercoaster ride.

Her spiritual side is very important to her; she has a passion for the healing modality of mindset, wellbeing, and meditation. She is in her element when she is in her happy place in nature, the peaceful sound of the ocean, sitting in her Zen Garden or her sensory room. This is where she is reminded of gratitude for everything she has experienced and everything she now has in her life.

The very raw and honest lessons in her chapter are written as not only an awakening and awareness for herself but for others.

Dawn is very outgoing. She attributes her friendliness to a country upbringing and always likes to see the best in everyone and every challenge that life has thrown her. Her health issues have given her opportunities to put into practice the tools she has learned over the years through a range of self-development courses. She credits being a Diversional Therapist, and her mindfulness and life coaching training, with reducing her stress levels over the past few years.

Dawn's take-away from her journey for all women is: NEVER disregard symptoms, no matter how slight. Know your body, and never be afraid to ask for a second opinion. It was the willingness of Gillian, her Melbourne GP, to look beyond the obvious that saved Dawn's life.

Heather Thorne

Heather was born in Perth, Western Australia and moved to Melbourne in April 2018. She has a younger sister still living in Perth and two adult daughters in Melbourne.

After leaving school, she studied secondary school teaching, following in her mother's footsteps.

In 2004, Heather's mother was diagnosed with Alzheimer's disease. She lived with it for fifteen years, the last eleven in residential care. In the process of learning what she could about the illness and how to care for her mother, Heather learned that the risk of dementia could be reduced by changing lifestyle habits. She decided that this was information that everyone needed to have.

This led her to undertake a Bachelor of Preventive Health (Health Promotion) at the University of Notre Dame. While studying, she landed her dream job with Alzheimer's Australia WA, educating the community about brain health and reducing the risk of dementia.

This is her way of making a positive difference to the quality of care older people receive.

In 2021, Heather completed an International TESOL Certificate and is a specialist English teacher for the aged care sector. She helps personal care workers improve their English to work in residential and community settings.

She can be contacted by email at:
agedcareenglishservices@gmail.com

Caterina Zanca

Constantly bullied at school and enduring many years of harassment from various family members, Caterina Zanca struggled with her weight for as long as she can remember.

Caterina has now put the many years of yo-yo dieting and the many personal challenges and upheavals behind her. She has changed her negative mindset into positive self-thought and feels more focused than ever before. She has committed to changing her eating habits for life.

With the completion of a recent Weight Loss Consultancy course, Caterina feels empowered and equipped to share her knowledge and help people come to terms with their own weight issues.

Your weight does not define who you are, but unfortunately, other people sometimes use our weaknesses, such as our weight, to hurt us – but only if we allow them to do so.

Caterina hopes that her story will inspire others to achieve their own personal goals, and more importantly, teach the value of being kind and understanding towards each other.

Other Books By The Authors

Your Thoughts Matter: The Future You Are Creating Starts Now

By Antoinette Pellegrini (2017)

Reflections and Affirmations on connection and the power of positive thinking and conscious choice. The series is designed to inspire the reader to create the life they would love to live. Available at all major online retailers and at:

www.antoinettepellegrini.com

www.thethoughtconnection.com

Your Thoughts Matter Reflection Journal

Your Thoughts Matter Affirmation Cards

By Antoinette Pellegrini (2017)

Accompaniments to the book *Your Thoughts Matter: The Future You Are Creating Starts Now*. The Journal and Affirmation Cards are designed to assist the reader to integrate the learnings into their lives.

Available at:

www.antoinettepellegrini.com

www.thethoughtconnection.com

Live Your Truth
Book 1: We Inspire Now Series

Created by Antoinette Pellegrini (2018)

Co-Authors:
Antoinette Pellegrini and Diane Psaila

Ten authors share their stories about overcoming hardships and difficulties to pursue their goals, discover who they are and live their own truth.

Available at all major online retailers and at
www.antoinettepellegrini.com

www.weinspirenowbooks.com

A Message To Your Younger Self
Book 2: We Inspire Now Series

Created by Antoinette Pellegrini (2020)

Co-Authors:
Antoinette Pellegrini and Diane Psaila

Ten authors share the messages, words of advice and wisdom that they would give their younger selves. It is a book about healing and love - healing the past, taking that healing into the present, and loving the person you were and are today.

Available at all major online retailers and at www.antoinettepellegrini.com

www.weinspirenowbooks.com

Change Makers

Co- Author: Sal Prothero

Twenty four inspirational women share what drives their vision to serve others, create businesses and enrich lives in their communities and around the globe. Their unique stories will inspire you to push through your limitations until your own vision for impact becomes a reality.

Printed Copy: https://www.wholefoodnutrition.com.au/product/change-makers/

Kindle version: https://www.amazon.com.au/dp/B08BXW8CQ8

www.ingramcontent.com/pod-product-compliance
Lightning Source LLC
Chambersburg PA
CBHW050307010526
44107CB00055B/2135